ZUNI FETISHES

by Frank Hamilton Cushing

Introduction by Tom Bahti

Eighth Printing, 1988

FACSIMILE EDITION BY
KC PUBLICATIONS
LAS VEGAS, NEVADA

The text by Frank Hamilton Cushing is reproduced from the Second Annual Report of the Bureau of Ethnology as submitted to the Secretary of the Smithsonian Institution, 1880-81 by J. W. Powell, Director. The original volume was printed in 1883 by the Government Printing Office, Washington, D.C.

The work is reprinted in its original form using the same page and plate numbers. Of the three color plates in the volume, numbers I and XI are used on the front and back covers of this reprint. All color plates are reproduced in black and white throughout the edition

Tom Bahti, a graduate of the Anthropology Department of the University of New Mexico, was a dealer and collector of Indian art for many years. Well-known in his field, he served numerous times as a judge at exhibits of Southwestern Indian arts and crafts, wrote articles and lectured on the subject. He authored "Southwestern Indian Arts and Crafts," "Southwestern Indian Tribes," and "Southwestern Indian Ceremonials" published by KC Publications.

Mr. Bahti's interest in southwestern tribes was not limited to their crafts, however, as he also actively served several organizations whose goal was to improve the general welfare of the Indians through self-help programs.

THREE DOLLARS

Library of Congress number 66-23329
Published by KC Publications
Box 14883· Las Vegas, NV 89114
Printed in Korea

INTRODUCTION

This is probably not the place to ponder the shortcomings of our own white American society which leads so many of its members to seek the amulets and charms of cultures other than their own for the purpose of "warding off evil" and "bringing good luck". Nevertheless, aside from a serious interest by collectors, it is this very phenomena that has prompted to a great extent the reprinting of this article on Zuni fetishes[1] by Frank H. Cushing.[2]

The use of fetishes by Indians dates from pre-Columbian times[3] but their use is probably as prevalent today as it was in the past, for man's desire to control those forces beyond his immediate power has not lessened.

All tribes in the Southwest make and use fetishes but the pueblo Indians have developed them to the greatest degree. Of the pueblo tribes the Zuni have the reputation for being the most skillful at carving them. For this reason the Zunis are looked to as a source for personal charms and amulets by members of other tribes. The Navajos, for example, will barter for the figures of horses, cattle, sheep or goats to keep their herds and flocks free from disease and to insure their propagation. Small cylindrical pieces carved from banded calcite are also purchased for use as prayer sticks.

Fetishes may be of almost any form or material. The *mili*, a representation of the "Breath of Life" as given by Awonawilona, the Supreme Being of the Zunis, is a perfect ear of corn, filled with the seeds of sacred plants, wrapped in buckskin and set in a base of basketry and covered with the feathers of various birds. *Ettone*, a fetish of the Rain Priests which symbolizes Mother Earth, rain and all of the life-giving forces upon which man depends, consists of short sections of painted reed filled with seeds and water (One contains a live toad[4]) and wrap-

---

[1] Fetish and fetich are both correct; fetish is now the preferred spelling.

[2] Frank H. Cushing (born 1857, died 1900) was a member of an expedition to the pueblo of Zuni in 1879 sent by Major J. W. Powell, Director of the Bureau of American Ethnology, Washington, D.C. Cushing remained with the Zunis for several years, writing numerous and excellent accounts of many aspects of their culture. He not only learned to speak the Zuni language but lived, as nearly as possible, as a Zuni. So well was he accepted by these people that he was given a Zuni name (Medicine Flower) and initiated into the Bow Priesthood as a War Chief. Because of his habit of dressing in a dandifield version of a Zuni warrior the Indians nicknamed him "Many Buttons", a reference to his overuse of silver decorations.

[3] The meanings of many of the words used in songs and prayers relating to fetishes are unknown today, an indication of an early origin of the use of fetishes.

[4] Stevenson, Matilde Coxe., p. 163 "The Zuni Indians" 23rd Annual Report, Bureau of American Ethnology, Washington, D.C. 1904.

ped with cotton cord. Tied to this bundle is an arrowhead and several beads.

Concretions, plant or animal material, and of course carvings in shell, stone or wood can all be used as fetishes but their purpose remains the same: to assist man, that most vulnerable of all living creatures, in meeting the problems that face him during his life. Each fetish contains a living power, which, if treated properly and with veneration will give its help to its owner. Should a desired result fail to be attained the fetish is not at fault but the person who conducted the ceremony is. Either he offended the fetish (perhaps by failing to feed it ceremonially) or was not of "good heart" when he asked for its assistance.

A fetish may be owned by an individual, clan, secret society or it may be regarded as the property of the entire tribe and its care entrusted to a responsible member of the group. Because the power of a fetish is regarded as a living thing it must be carefully tended and ceremonially fed, usually with corn meal. When not in use they are kept in special fetish jars.

The purposes for which fetishes may be used are varied: hunting, diagnosing and curing diseases, initiations, war, gambling, propagation, witchcraft, and detection and protection against witchcraft.

Hunting fetishes[5] of the kind that would be the property of an individual are the ones most frequently seen for sale. Aside from age, which is seldom obvious, there is not essential difference between a new and an old fetish. The "antiquing" of new fetishes is practiced occasionally but only because of the gullibility of the average non-Indian collector who is inclined to believe that age can be directly equated with quality and value.[6]

Because of the demand by collectors a number of facsimile reproductions of clan or society fetishes (referred to by the trade as "Kiva fetishes") are produced. Usually carved from an antler they often represent the Feathered Serpent, mountain lion or wolf and are elaborately decorated with hair, feathers, shell, turquoise, coral and arrowpoints.

In addition to fetishes Zuni craftsmen also produce a large number of animals and birds that are not used as fetishes. The so-called fetish necklace, figurines of rabbits, owls, dogs and humans, fall into this category.

---

[5] The use of fetishes of prey is not limited to the chase; these same pieces may be used for "seeing disease" (diagnosis) or curing certain maladies. The hunter of the underworld — the mole or shrew — is used to protect crops against rodents.

[6] The fetish most highly prized by a Zuni is the natural concretion that bears a resemblance to an animal. Most non-Indians would regard such an item merely as a curiosity.

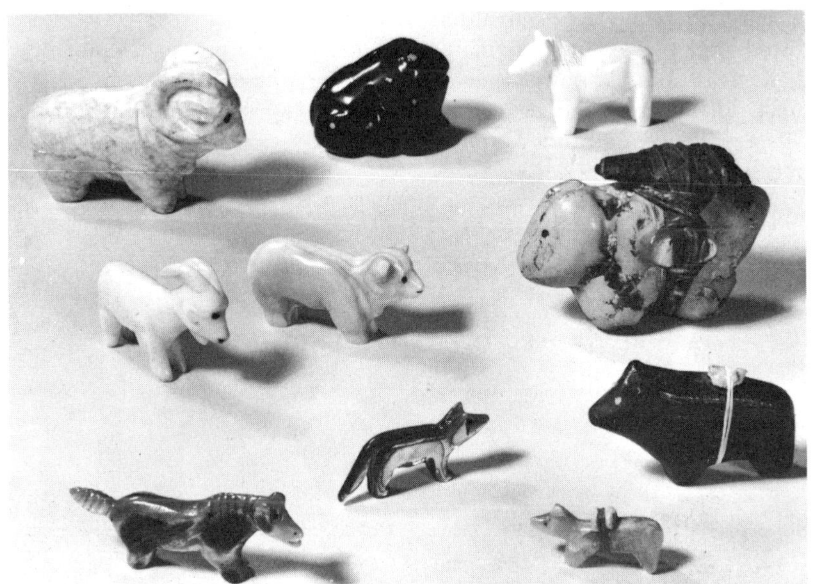

Modern Zuni fetishes.

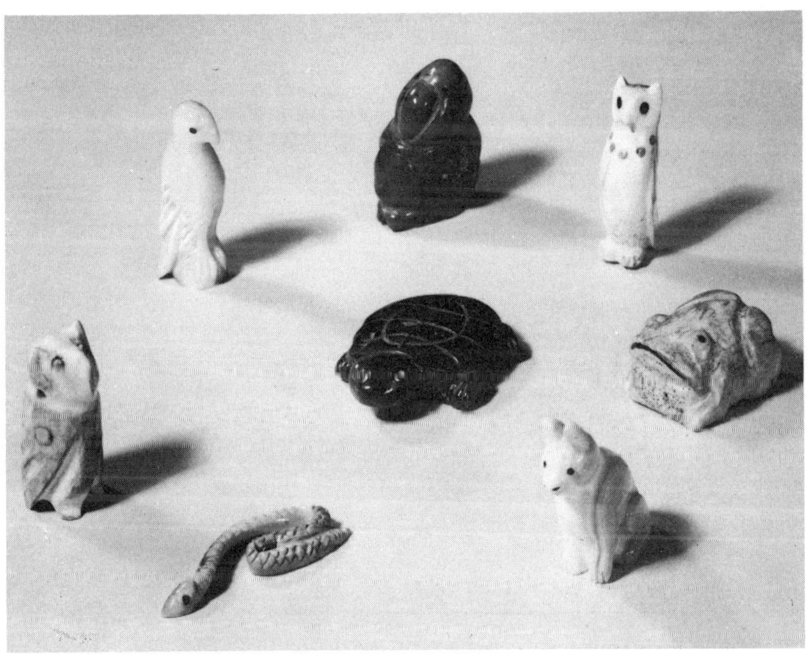

Carvings in stone, shell and antler represent animals but are not used as fetishes.

The difference between a fetish and a carving (other than those listed above) is purely a matter of belief. If a particular object is believed to possess power then it is a fetish.[7] The collector is interested in form, material and age of a fetish; the Indian is interested in its efficacy. These attitudes are culturally determined and not easily reconciled.

Tom Bahti
Tucson, 1966

SELECTED REFERENCES

BAHTI, TOM, *"Southwestern Indian Arts & Crafts"*, KC Publications, Box 14883, Las Vegas, Nevada 89114.

BAHTI, TOM, *"Southwestern Indian Ceremonials"*, KC Publications, Box 14883, Las Vegas, Nevada 89114.

STEVENSON, MATILDE C., *"The Zuni Indians"* 23rd. Annual Report, Bureau of American Ethnology, Washington, D.C. 1904.

KIRK, RUTH F., *"Introduction to Zuni Fetishism"*, Volume numbers 6, 7, 8, 9, 10. El Palacio, Santa Fe, New Mexico. June-October 1943.

KLUCKHOHN, CLYDE, *"Navajo Witchcraft"*. Beacon Press, Boston, Massachusetts, 1966.

LANGE, CHARLES H., *"Cochiti"*, University of Texas Press, Austin, Texas. 1959.

---

[7] The writer has seen cut glass chandelier "crystals" in a medicine bundle that were used for predicting the weather and a well-worn dime store rubber mouse included as part of a medicine man's paraphernalia.

ZUÑI FETICHES.

BY FRANK H. CUSHING.

ZUÑI PHILOSOPHY.

The Á-shi-wi, or Zuñis, suppose the sun, moon, and stars, the sky, earth, and sea, in all their phenomena and elements; and all inanimate objects, as well as plants, animals, and men, to belong to one great system of all-conscious and interrelated life, in which the degrees of relationship seem to be determined largely, if not wholly, by the degrees of resemblance. In this system of life the starting point is man, the most finished, yet the lowest organism; at least, the lowest because most dependent and least mysterious. In just so far as an organism, actual or imaginary, resembles his, is it believed to be related to him and correspondingly mortal; in just so far as it is mysterious, is it considered removed from him, further advanced, powerful, and immortal. It thus happens that the animals, because alike mortal and endowed with similar physical functions and organs, are considered more nearly related to man than are the gods; more nearly related to the gods than is man, because more mysterious, and characterized by specific instincts and powers which man does not of himself possess. Again, the elements and phenomena of nature, because more mysterious, powerful and immortal, seem more closely related to the higher gods than are the animals; more closely related to the animals than are the higher gods, because their manifestations often resemble the operations of the former.

In consequence of this, and through the confusion of the subjective with the objective, any element or phenomenon in nature, which is believed to possess a personal existence, is endowed with a personality analogous to that of the animal whose operations most resemble its manifestation. For instance, lightning is often given the form of a serpent, with or without an arrow-pointed tongue, because its course through the sky is serpentine, its stroke instantaneous and destructive; yet it is named Wí-lo-lo-a-ne, a word derived not from the name of the serpent itself, but from that of its most obvious trait, its gliding, zigzag motion. For this reason, the serpent is supposed to be more nearly related to lightning than to man; more nearly related to man than is lightning, because mortal and less mysterious. As further illustrative of the interminable relationships which are established on resemblances fancied or actual, the flint arrow-point may be cited. Although fashioned by man, it is regarded as originally the gift or "flesh" of lightning, as made by the power of lightning, and rendered more effective by these connections with the dread element; pursuant of which idea, the zigzag or lightning marks are added to the shafts of arrows. A chapter might be written concerning this idea, which may possibly help to explain the Celtic, Scandinavian, and Japanese beliefs concerning "elf-shafts," and "thunder-stones," and "bolts."

In like manner, the supernatural beings of man's fancy—the "master existences"—are supposed to be more nearly related to the personalities with which the elements and phenomena of nature are endowed than to either animals or men; because, like those elements and phenomena, and unlike men and animals, they are connected with remote tradition in a manner identical with their supposed existence to-day, and therefore are considered immortal.

To the above descriptions of the supernatural beings of Zuñi Theology should be added the statement that all of these beings are given the forms either of animals, of monsters compounded of man and beast, or of man. The animal gods comprise by far the largest class.

In the Zuñi, no general name is equivalent to "the gods," unless it be the two expressions which relate only to the higher or creating and controlling beings—the "causes," Creators and Masters, "Pí-kwain=á-hâ-i" (Surpassing Beings), and "Á-tä-tchu" (All-fathers), the beings superior to all others in wonder and power, and the "Makers" as well as the "Finishers" of existence. These last are classed with the supernatural beings, personalities of nature, object beings, etc., under one term—

a. Í-shothl-ti-mon=á-hâ-i, from *í-shothl-ti-mo-na*=ever recurring, immortal, and *á-hâ-i*=beings.

Likewise, the animals and animal gods, and sometimes even the supernatural beings, having animal or combined animal and human personalities, are designated by one term only—

b. K'ia-pin=á-hâ-i, from *k'ia-pin-na*=raw, and *á-hâ-i*=beings. Of these, however, three divisions are made:

(1.) K'ia-pin-á-hâ-i=game animals, specifically applied to those animals furnishing flesh to man.

(2.) K'iä-shem-á-hâ-i, from *k'iä-we*=water, *she-man*=wanting, and *á-hâ-i*=beings, the water animals, specially applied not only to them, but also to all animals and animal gods supposed to be associated sacredly with water, and through which water is supplicated.

(3.) Wé-ma-á-hâ-i, from *we-ma*=prey, and *á-hâ-i*=beings, "Prey Beings," applied alike to the prey animals and their representatives among the gods. Finally we have the terms—

c. Ak-na=á-hâ-i, from *ák-na*=done, cooked, or baked, ripe, and *á-hâ-i*= beings, the "Done Beings," referring to mankind; and *d.* Äsh-i-k'ia=á-hâ-i, from *ä'sh-k'ia*=made, finished, and *á-hâ-i*=beings, "Finished Beings," including the *dead* of mankind.

That very little distinction is made between these orders of life, or that they are at least closely related, seems to be indicated by the absence from the entire language of any general term for *God.* True, there are many beings in Zuñi Mythology godlike in attributes, anthropomorphic, monstrous, and elemental, which are known as the "Finishers or makers of the paths of life," while the most superior of all is called the "Holder of the paths (of our lives)," Hâ'-no-o-na wí-la-po-na. Not only these gods, but all supernatural beings, men, animals, plants, and many objects in nature, are regarded as personal existences, and are included in the one term *á-hâ-i*, from *á*, the plural particle signifying "all," and *hâ-i*, being or life,="Life," "the Beings." This again leads us to the important and interesting conclusion that all beings, whether deistic and supernatural, or animistic and mortal, are regarded as belonging to one system; and that they are likewise believed to be related by blood seems to be indicated by the fact that human beings are spoken of as the "children of men," while *all* other beings are referred to as "the Fathers," the "All-fathers," and "Our Fathers."

THE WORSHIP OF ANIMALS.

It naturally follows from the Zuñi's philosophy of life, that his worship, while directed to the more mysterious and remote powers of nature, or, as he regards them, existences, should relate more especially to the animals; that, in fact, the animals, as more nearly related to himself than are these existences, more nearly related to these existences than to himself, should be frequently made to serve as mediators between them and him. We find this to be the case. It follows likewise that in his inability to differentiate the objective from the subjective, he should establish relationships between natural objects which resemble animals and the animals themselves; that he should even ultimately imitate these animals for the sake of establishing such relationships, using such accidental resemblances as his *motives*, and thus developing a conventionality in all art connected with his worship. It follows that the special requirements of his life or of the life of his ancestors should influence him to select as his favored mediators or aids those animals which seemed best fitted, through peculiar characteristics and powers, to meet these requirements. This, too, we find to be the case, for, preeminently a man of war and the chase, like all savages, the Zuñi has chosen above all other animals those which supply him with food and useful material, together with the animals which prey on them, giving preference to the latter. Hence, while the name of the former class is applied preferably as a *general* term to all animals and animal gods, as previously explained, the name of the latter is used with equal preference as a term for all fetiches (Wé-ma-we), whether of the prey animals themselves or of other animals and beings. Of course it is equally natural, since they are connected with man both in the scale of being and in the power to supply his physical wants more nearly than are the higher gods, that the animals or animal gods should greatly outnumber and even give character to all others. We find that the Fetiches of the Zuñis relate mostly to the animal gods, and principally to the prey gods.

ORIGIN OF ZUÑI FETICHISM.

This fetichism seems to have arisen from the relationships heretofore alluded to, and to be founded on the myths which have been invented to account for those relationships. It is therefore not surprising that those fetiches most valued by the Zuñis should be either natural concretions (Plate I, Fig. 6), or objects in which the evident original resemblance to animals has been only heightened by artificial means (Plate IV, Fig. 7; Plate V, Fig. 4; Plate VI, Figs. 3, 6, 8; Plate VIII, Figs. 1, 3, 4, 5; Plate IX, Fig. 1).

Another highly prized class of fetiches are, on the contrary, those which are elaborately carved, but show evidence, in their polish and dark patina, of great antiquity. They are either such as have been found by the Zuñis about pueblos formerly inhabited by their ancestors or are tribal possessions which have been handed down from generation to generation, until their makers, and even the fact that they were made by any member of the tribe, have been forgotten. It is supposed by the priests (Á-shi-wa-ni) of Zuñi that not only these, but all true fetiches, are either actual petrifactions of the animals they represent, or were such originally. Upon this supposition is founded the following tradition, taken, as are others to follow, from a remarkable mythologic epic, which I have entitled the Zuñi Iliad.

THE ZUÑI ILIAD.

Although oral, this epic is of great length, metrical, rythmical even in parts, and filled with archaic expressions nowhere to be found in the modern Zuñi. It is to be regretted that the original diction cannot here be preserved. I have been unable, however, to record literally even portions of this piece of aboriginal literature, as it is jealously guarded by the priests, who are its keepers, and is publicly repeated by them only once in four years, and then only in the presence of the priests of the various orders. As a member of one of the latter, I was enabled to

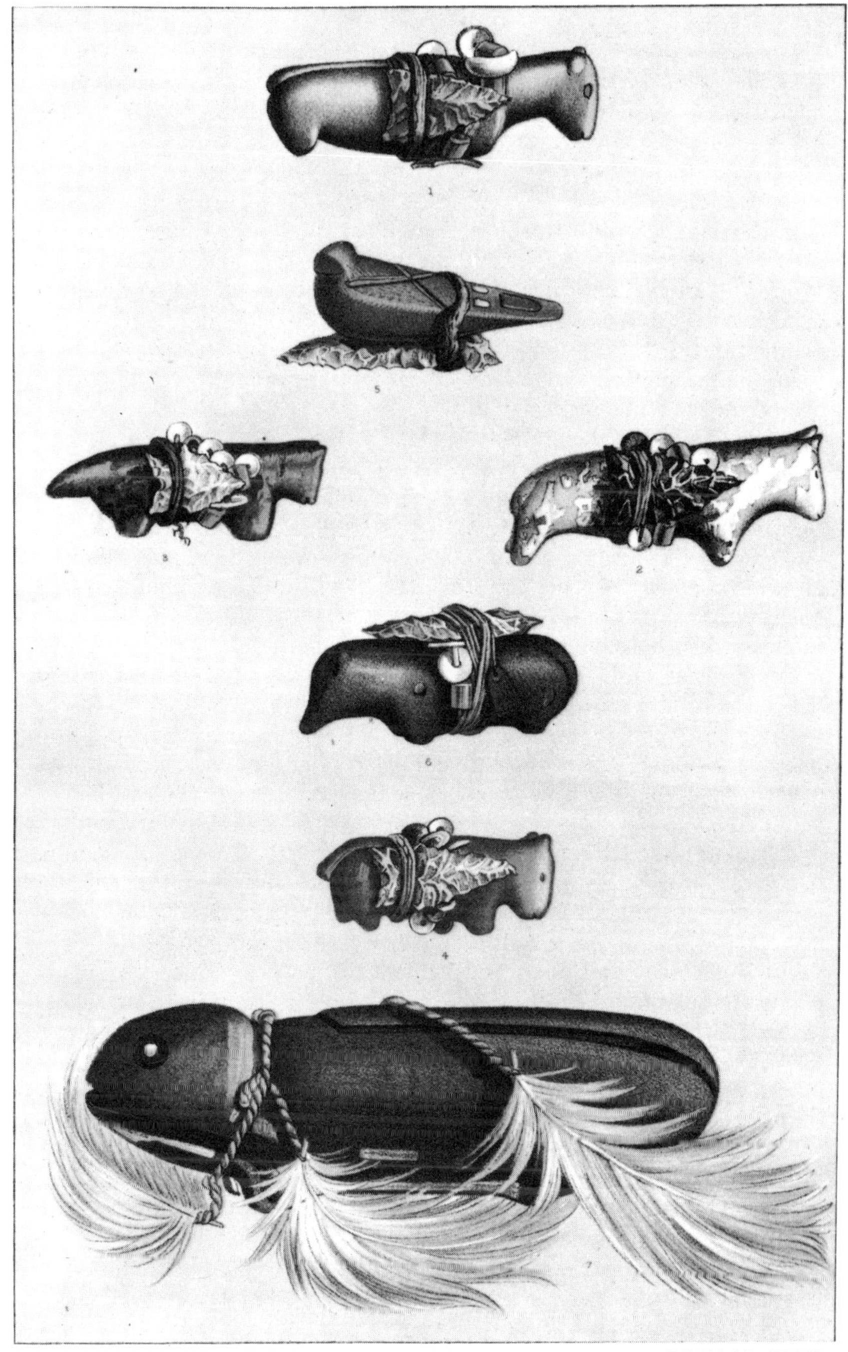

T. Sinclair & Son, lith., Phila.

PREY GOD FETICHES.

listen to one-fourth of it during the last recitation, which occurred in February, 1881. I therefore give mere abstracts, mostly furnished from memory, and greatly condensed, but pronounced correct, so far as they go, by one of the above-mentioned priests.

THE DRYING OF THE WORLD.

In the days when all was new, men lived in the four caverns of the lower regions (Á-wi-tĕn té-huthl-na-kwĭn=the "Four Wombs of the World"). In the lowermost one of these men first came to know of their existence. It was dark, and as men increased they began to crowd one another and were very unhappy. Wise men came into existence among them, whose children supplicated them that they should obtain deliverance from such a condition of life.

It was then that the "Holder of the Paths of Life," the Sun-father, created from his own being two children, who fell to earth for the good of all beings (Ú-a-nam átch-pi-ah-k'oa). The Sun-father endowed these children with immortal youth, with power even as his own power, and created for them a bow (Á-mi-to-lan-ne,= the Rain Bow) and an arrow (Wí-lo-lo-a-ne, = Lightning). For them he made also a shield like unto his own, of magic power, and a knife of flint, the great magic war knife (Sá-wa-ni-k'ia ä'-tchi-ë-ne). The shield (Pí-al-lan-ne) was a mere network of sacred cords (Pí-tsau-pi-wi, = cotton) on a hoop of wood, and to the center of this net-shield was attached the magic knife.

These children cut the face of the world with their magic knife, and were borne down upon their shield into the caverns in which all men dwelt. There, as the leaders of men, they lived with their children, mankind.

They listened to the supplications of the priests. They built a ladder to the roof of the first cave and widened with their flint knife and shield the aperture through which they had entered. Then they led men forth into the second cavern, which was larger and not quite so dark.

Ere long men multiplied and bemoaned their condition as before. Again they besought their priests, whose supplications were once more listened to by the divine children. As before, they led all mankind into the third world. Here it was still larger and like twilight, for the light of the Sun himself sifted down through the opening. To these poor creatures (children) of the dark the opening itself seemed a blazing sun.

But as time went on men multiplied even as they had before, and at last, as at first, bemoaned their condition. Again the two children listened to their supplications, and it was then that the children of men first saw the light of their father, the Sun.

The world had been covered with water. It was damp and unstable. Earthquakes disturbed its surface. Strange beings rose up through it, monsters and animals of prey. As upon an island in the middle of a great water, the children of men were led forth into the light of their father, the Sun. It blinded and heated them so that they cried to one another in anguish, and fell down, and covered their eyes with their bare hands and arms, for men were black then, like the caves they came from, and naked, save for a covering at the loins of rush, like yucca fiber, and sandals of the same, and their eyes, like the owl's, were unused to the daylight.

Eastward the two children began to lead them, toward the Home of the Sun-father.

Now, it happened that the two children saw that the earth must be dried and hardened, for wherever the foot touched the soil water gathered—as may be seen even in the rocks to-day—and the monsters which rose forth from the deep devoured the children of men. Therefore they consulted together and sought the advice of their creator, the Sun-father. By his directions, they placed their magic shield upon the wet earth. They drew four lines a step apart upon the soft sands. Then the older brother said to the younger, "Wilt thou, or shall I, take the lead?"

"I will take the lead," said the younger.

"Stand thou upon the last line," said the older.

And when they had laid upon the magic shield the rainbow, and across it the arrows of lightning, toward all the quarters of the world, the younger brother took his station facing toward the right. The older brother took his station facing toward the left. When all was ready, both braced themselves to run. The older brother drew his arrow to the head, let fly, and struck the rainbow and the lightning arrows midway, where they crossed. Instantly, *thlu-tchu!* shot the arrows of lightning in every direction, and fire rolled over the face of the earth, and the two gods followed the courses of their arrows of lightning.

Now that the surface of the earth was hardened, even the animals of prey, powerful and like the fathers (gods) themselves, would have devoured the children of men; and the Two thought it was not well that they should all be permitted to live, "for," said they, "alike will the children of men and the children of the animals of prey multiply themselves. The animals of prey are provided with talons and teeth; men are but poor, the finished beings of earth, therefore the weaker."

Whenever they came across the pathway of one of these animals, were he great mountain lion or but a mere mole, they struck him with the fire of lightning which they carried in their magic shield. *Thlu!* and instantly he was shriveled and burnt into stone.

Then said they to the animals that they had thus changed to stone, "That ye may not be evil unto men, but that ye may be a great good unto them, have we changed you into rock everlasting. By the magic breath of prey, by the heart that shall endure forever within you, shall ye be made to serve instead of to devour mankind."

Thus was the surface of the earth hardened and scorched and many of all kinds of beings changed to stone. Thus, too, it happens that we find, here and there throughout the world, their forms, sometimes large like the beings themselves, sometimes shriveled and distorted. And we often see among the rocks the forms of many beings that live no longer, which shows us that all was different in the " days of the new."

Of these petrifactions, which are of course mere concretions or strangely eroded rock-forms, the Zuñis say, " Whomsoever of us may be met with the light of such great good fortune may *see* (discover, find) them and should treasure them for the sake of the sacred (magic) power which was given them in the days of the new. For the spirits of the We-ma-á-hâ-i still live, and are pleased to receive from us the Sacred Plume (of the heart—Lä-sho-a-ni), and sacred necklace of treasure (Thlâ-thle-a); hence they turn their ears and the ears of their brothers in our direction that they may hearken to our prayers (sacred talks) and know our wants."

POWER OF THE FETICHES.

This tradition not only furnishes additional evidence relative to the preceding statements, but also, taken in connection with the following belief, shows quite clearly to the native wherein lies the power of his fetiches. It is supposed that the hearts of the great animals of prey are infused with a spirit or medicine of magic influence over the hearts of the animals they prey upon, or the game animals (K'ia-pin-á-hâ-i); that their breaths (the "Breath of Life"—Hâ-i-an-pi-nan-ne—and soul are synonymous in Zuñi Mythology), derived from their hearts, and breathed upon their prey, whether near or far, never fail to overcome them, piercing their hearts and causing their limbs to stiffen, and the animals themselves to lose their strength. Moreover, the roar or cry of a beast of prey is accounted its Sá-wa-ni-k'ia, or magic medicine of destruction, which, heard by the game animals, is fatal to them, because it charms their senses, as does the breath their hearts. Since the mountain lion, for example, lives by the blood ("life fluid") and flesh of the game animals, and by these alone, he is endowed not only with the above powers, but with peculiar powers in the senses of sight and smell. Moreover, these powers, as derived from his heart, are preserved in his fetich, since his heart still lives, even though his person be changed to stone.

PREY GODS OF THE SIX REGIONS.

THEIR ORIGIN.

Therefore it happens that the use of these fetiches is chiefly connected with the chase. To this, however, there are some exceptions. One of these may be partly explained by the following myth concerning Pó-shai-aŋ-k'ia, the God (Father) of the Medicine societies or sacred esoteric orders, of which there are twelve in Zuñi, and others among the different pueblo tribes. He is supposed to have appeared in human form, poorly clad, and therefore reviled by men; to have taught the ancestors of the Zuñi, Taos, Oraibi, and Coçonino Indians their agricultural and other arts, their systems of worship by means of plumed and painted prayer-sticks; to have organized their medicine societies; and then to have disappeared toward his home in Shí-pä-pu-li-ma (from *shí-pi-a*=mist, vapor; *u-lin*=surrounding; and *i-mo-na*=sitting place of—"The mist-enveloped city"), and to have vanished beneath the world, whence he is said to have departed for the home of the Sun. He is still the conscious auditor of the prayers of his children, the invisible ruler of the spiritual Shí-pä-pu-li-ma, and of the lesser gods of the medicine orders, the principal "Finisher of the Paths of our Lives." He is, so far as any identity can be established, the "Montezuma" of popular and usually erroneous Mexican tradition.

PÓ-SHAI-AŊ-K'IA.

In ancient times, while yet all beings belonged to one family, Pó-shai-aŋ-k'ia, the father of our sacred bands, lived with his children (disciples) in the City of the Mists, the middle place (center) of the Medicine societies of the world. There he was guarded on all sides by his six warriors, Á-pi-thlan shí-wa-ni (*pí-thlan*=bow, *shí-wa-ni*=priests), the prey gods; toward the North by the Mountain Lion (Long Tail); toward the West by the Bear (Clumsy Foot); toward the South by the Badger (Black Mark Face); toward the East by the Wolf (Hang Tail); above by the Eagle (White Cap); and below by the Mole. When he was about to go forth into the world, he divided the universe into six regions, namely, the North (Pï'sh-lan-kwïn táh-na=Direction of the Swept or Barren place); the West (K'iä'-li-shi-ïn-kwïn táh-na=Direction of the Home of the Waters); the South (Á-la-ho-ïn-kwïn táh-na=Direction of the Place of the Beautiful Red); the East (Té-lu-a-ïn-kwïn táh-na=Direction of the Home of Day); the Upper Regions (Í-ya-ma-ïn-kwïn táh-na=Direction of the Home of the High); and the Lower Regions (Ma-ne-lam-ïn-kwïn táh-na=Direction of the Home of the Low)."

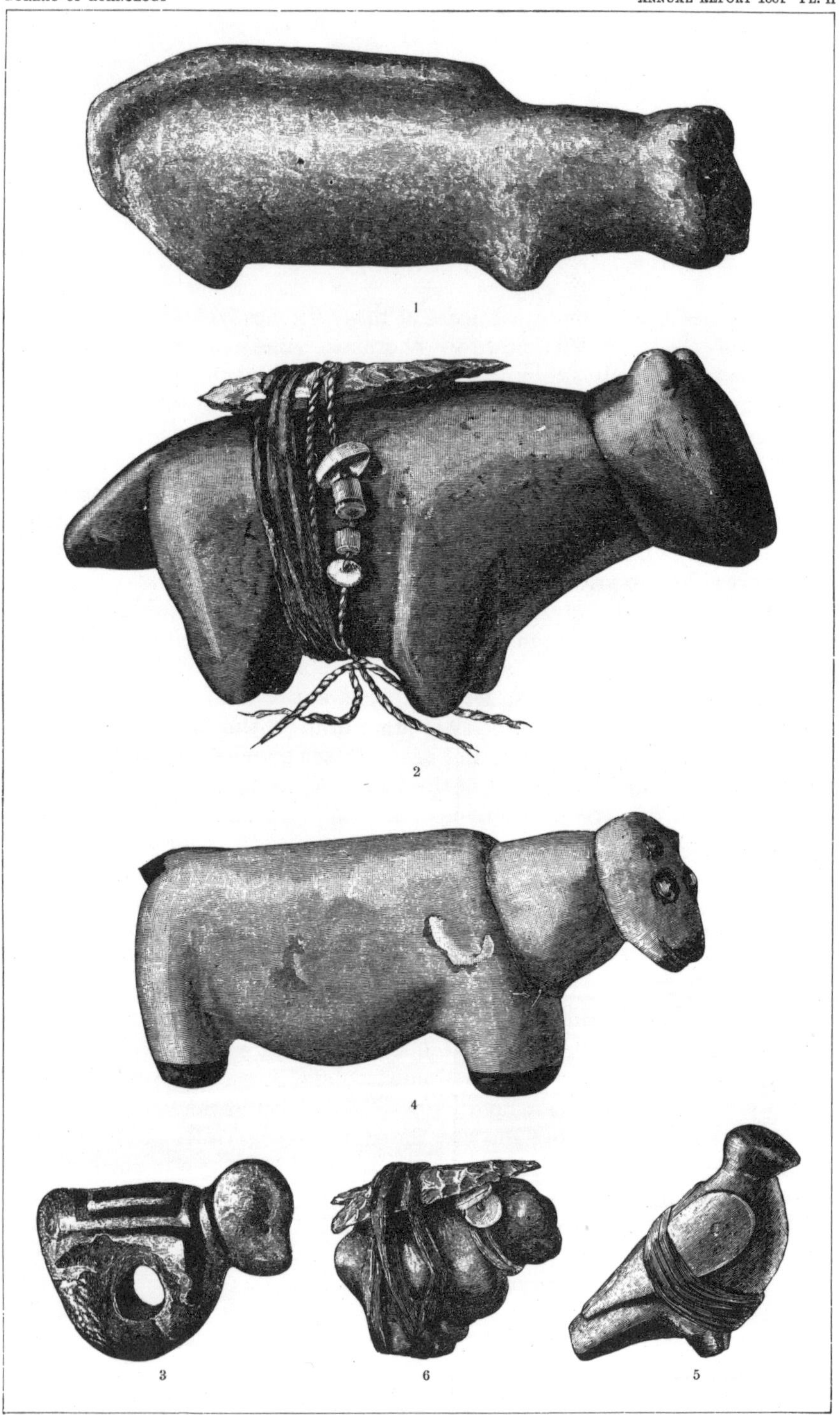

PREY GOD FETICHES OF THE SIX REGIONS.

All, save the first of these terms, are archaic. The modern names for the West, South, East, Upper and Lower Regions signifying respectively—"The Place of Evening," "The Place of the Salt Lake" (Las Salinas), "The Place whence comes the Day," "The Above," and "The Below."

In the center of the great sea of each of these regions stood a very ancient sacred place (Té-thlä-shi-na-kwïn), a great mountain peak. In the North was the Mountain Yellow, in the West the Mountain Blue, in the South the Mountain Red, in the East the Mountain White, above the Mountain All-color, and below the Mountain Black.

We do not fail to see in this clear reference to the natural colors of the regions referred to—to the barren north and its auroral hues, the west with its blue Pacific, the rosy south, the white daylight of the east, the many hues of the clouded sky, and the black darkness of the "caves and holes of earth." Indeed, these colors are used in the pictographs and in all the mythic symbolism of the Zuñis, to indicate the directions or regions respectively referred to as connected with them.

Then said Pó-shai-aŋ-k'ia to the Mountain Lion (Plate II, Fig. 1), "Long Tail, thou art stout of heart and strong of will. Therefore give I unto thee and unto thy children forever the mastership of the gods of prey, and the guardianship of the great Northern World (for thy coat is of yellow), that thou guard from that quarter the coming of evil upon my children of men, that thou receive in that quarter their messages to me, that thou become the father in the North of the sacred medicine orders all, that thou become a Maker of the Paths (of men's lives)."

Thither went the Mountain Lion. Then said Pó-shai-aŋ-k'ia to the Bear (Plate II, Fig. 2), "Black Bear, thou art stout of heart and strong of will. Therefore make I thee the younger brother of the Mountain Lion, the guardian and master of the West, for thy coat is of the color of the land of night," etc.

To the Badger (Plate II, Fig. 3), "Thou art stout of heart but *not* strong of will. Therefore make I thee the younger brother of the Bear, the guardian and master of the South, for thy coat is ruddy and marked with black and white equally, the colors of the land of summer, which is red, and stands between the day and the night, and thy homes are on the sunny sides of the hills," etc.

To the White Wolf (Plate II, Fig. 4), "Thou art stout of heart and strong of will. Therefore make I thee the younger brother of the Badger, the guardian and master of the East, for thy coat is white and gray, the color of the day and dawn," etc.

And to the Eagle (Plate II, Fig. 5), he said: "White Cap (Bald Eagle), thou art passing stout of heart and strong of will. Therefore make I thee the younger brother of the Wolf, the guardian and master of the Upper regions, for thou fliest through the skies without tiring, and thy coat is speckled like the clouds," etc.

"Prey Mole (Plate II, Fig. 6), thou art stout of heart and strong of will. Therefore make I thee the younger brother of the Eagle, the guardian and master of the Lower regions, for thou burrowest through the earth without tiring, and thy coat is of black, the color of the holes and caves of earth," etc.

THEIR POWER AS MEDIATORS.

Thus it may be seen that all these animals are supposed to possess not only the guardianship of the six regions, but also the mastership, not merely geographic, but of the medicine powers, etc., which are supposed to emanate from them; that they are the mediators between men and Pó-shai-aŋ-ki'a, and conversely, between the latter and men.

As further illustrative of this relationship it may not be amiss to add that, aside from representing the wishes of men to Pó-shai-aŋ-k'ia, by means of the spirits of the prayer plumes, which, it is supposed, the prey gods take into his presence, and which are, as it were, memoranda (like *quippus*) to him and other high gods of the prayers of men, they are also made to bear messages to men from him and his associated gods.

For instance, it is believed that any member of the medicine orders who neglects his religious duties as such is rendered liable to punishment (Hä'-ti-a-k'ia-na-k'ia=reprehension) by Pó-shai-aŋ-k'ia through some one of his warriors.

As illustrative of this, the story of an adventure of Mí-tsi, an Indian who "still lives, but limps," is told by the priests with great emphasis to any backsliding member.

MÍ-TSI.

Mí-tsi was long a faithful member of the Little Fire order (Ma-ke-tsá-na-kwe), but he grew careless, neglected his sacrifices, and resigned his rank as "Keeper of the Medicines," from mere laziness. In vain his fathers warned him. He only grew hot with anger. One day Mí-tsi went up on the mesas to cut corral posts. He sat down to eat his dinner. A great black bear walked out of the thicket near at hand and leisurely approached him. Mí-tsi dropped his dinner and climbed a neighboring little dead pine tree. The bear followed him and climbed it, too. Mí-tsi began to have sad thoughts of the words of his fathers.

"Alas," he cried, "pity me, my father from the West-land!" In vain he promised to be a good Ma-ke-tsá-na-kwe. Had not Pó-shai-aŋ-k'ia commanded?

So the black bear seized him by the foot and pulled until Mí-tsi screamed from pain; but, cling as he would to the tree, the bear pulled him to the ground. Then he lay down on Mí-tsi and pressed the wind out of him so that he forgot. The black bear started to go; but eyed

Mí-tsi. Mí-tsi kicked. Black bear came and pressed his wind out again. It hurt Mí-tsi, and he said to himself, "Oh dear me! what shall I do? The father thinks I am not punished enough." So he kept very still. Black bear started again, then stopped and looked at Mí-tsi, started and stopped again, growled and moved off, for Mí-tsi kept very still. Then the black bear went slowly away, looking at Mí-tsi all the while, until he passed a little knoll. Mí-tsi crawled away and hid under a log. Then, when he thought himself man enough, he started for Zuñi. He was long sick, for the black bear had eaten his foot. He "still lives and limps," but he is a good Ma-ke-tsá-na-kwe. Who shall say that Pó-shai-aŋ-k'ia did not command?

THEIR WORSHIP.

The prey gods, through their relationship to Pó-shai-aŋ-k'ia, as "Makers of the Paths of Life," are given high rank among the gods. With this belief, their fetiches are held "as in captivity" by the priests of the various medicine orders, and greatly venerated by them as mediators between themselves and the animals they represent. In this character they are exhorted with elaborate prayers, rituals, and ceremonials. Grand sacrifices of plumed and painted prayer-sticks (Téthl-na-we) are made annually by the "Prey Brother Priesthood" (Wé-ma á-pa-pa á-shi-wa-ni) of these medicine societies, and at the full moon of each month lesser sacrifices of the same kind by the male members of the "Prey gentes" (Wé-ma á-no-ti-we) of the tribe.

PREY GODS OF THE HUNT.

THEIR RELATION TO THE OTHERS.

The fetich worship of the Zuñis naturally reaches its highest and most interesting development in its relationship to the chase, for the We-ma-á-hâ-i are considered *par excellence* the gods of the hunt. Of this class of fetiches, the special priests are the members of the "Great Coyote People" (Sá-ni-a-k'ia-kwe, or the Hunting Order), their keepers, the chosen members of the Eagle and Coyote gentes and of the Prey Brother priesthood.

The fetiches in question (Plate III) represent, with two exceptions, the same species of prey animals as those supposed to guard the six regions. These exceptions are, the Coyote (Sús-ki, Plate III, Fig. 2), which replaces the Black Bear of the West, and the Wild Cat (Té-pi, Plate III, Fig. 3), which takes the place of the Badger of the South.

In the prayer-songs of the Sá-ni-a-kía-kwe, the names of all of these prey gods are, with two exceptions, given in the language of the Rio Grande Indians. This is probably one of the many devices for securing greater secrecy, and rendering the ceremonials of the Hunter Society mysterious to other than members. The exceptions are, the Coyote, or Hunter god of the West, known by the archaic name of Thlä'-k'iä-tchu, instead of by its ordinary name of Sús-ki, and the Prey Mole or god of the Lower regions (Plate III, Fig. 5), which is named Maí-tu-pu, also archaic, instead of K'iä'-lu-tsi. Yet in most of the prayer and ritualistic recitals of this order all of these gods are spoken of by the names which distinguish them in the other orders of the tribe.

THEIR ORIGIN.

While all the prey gods of the hunt are supposed to have functions differing both from those of the six regions and those of the Priesthood of the Bow, spoken of further on, they are yet referred, like those of the first class, to special divisions of the world. In explanation of this, however, quite another myth is given. This myth, like the first, is derived from the epic before referred to, and occurs in the latter third of the long recital, where it pictures the tribes of the Zuñis, under the guidance of the Two Children, and the Kâ'-kâ at Kó-thlu-ël-lon-ne, now a marsh-bordered lagune situated on the eastern shore of the Colorado Chiquito, about fifteen miles north and west from the pueblo of

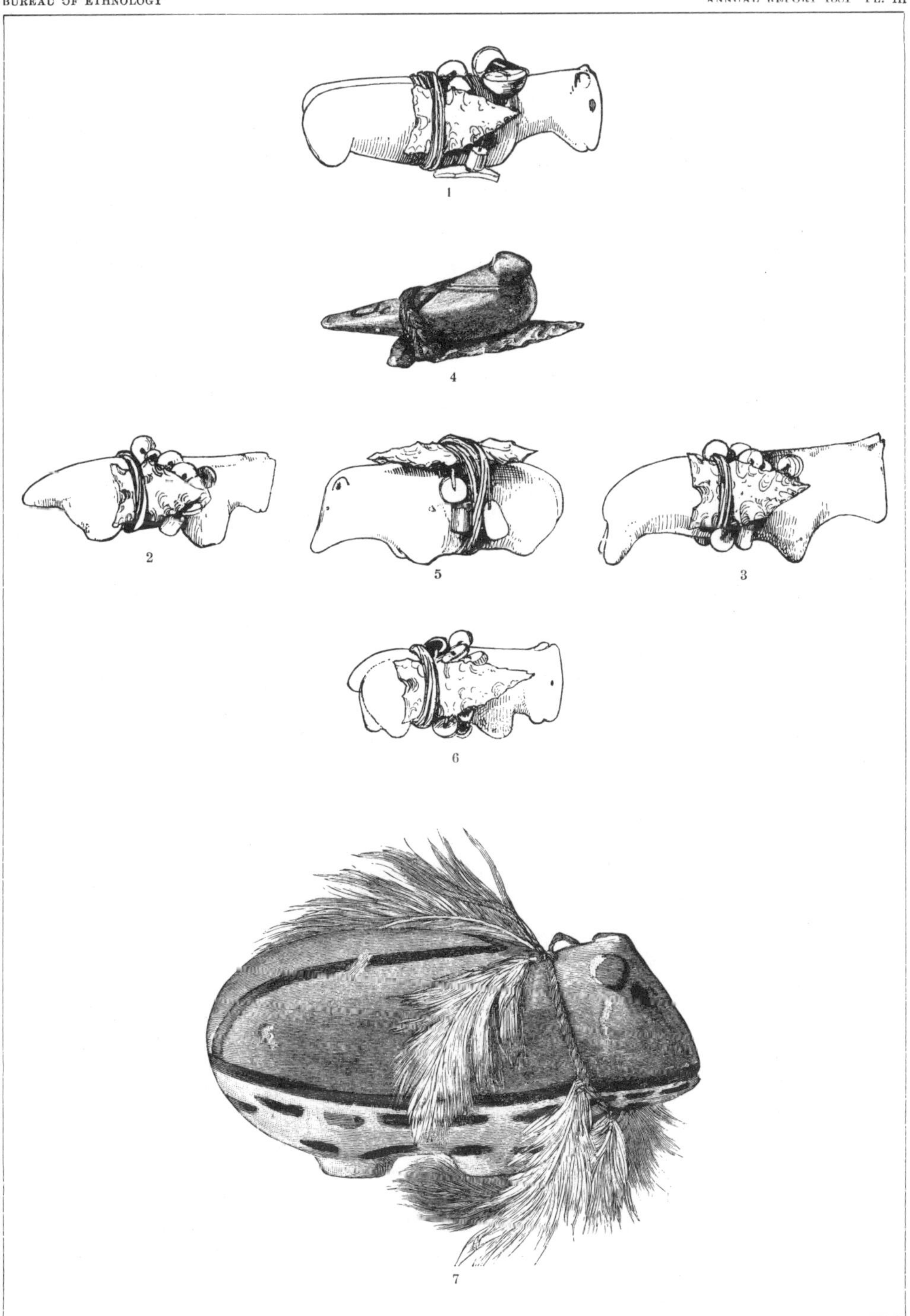

PREY GOD FETICHES OF THE HUNT.

San Juan, Arizona, and nearly opposite the mouth of the Rio Concho. This lagune is probably formed in the basin or crater of some extinct geyser or volcanic spring, as the two high and wonderfully similar mountains on either side are identical in formation with those in which occur the cave-craters farther south on the same river. It has, however, been largely filled in by the *débris* brought down by the Zuñi River, which here joins the Colorado Chiquito. Kó-thlu-ël-lon signifies the "standing place (city) of the Kâ'-kâ" (from *Kâ*=a contraction of Kâ'-kâ, the sacred dance, and *thlu-ël-lon*=standing place).

THE DISTRIBUTION OF THE ANIMALS.

Men began their journey from the Red River, and the Kâ'-kâ still lived, as it does now, at Kó-thlu-ël-lon-ne, when the wonderful Snail People (not snails, as may be inferred, but a tribe of that name), who lived in the "Place of the Snails" (K'iá-ma-k'ia-kwïn), far south of where Zuñi now is, caused, by means of their magic power, all the game animals in the whole world round about to gather together in the great forked cañon-valley under their town, and there to be hidden.

The walls of this cañon were high and insurmountable, and the whole valley although large was filled full of the game animals, so that their feet rumbled and rattled together like the sound of distant thunder, and their horns crackled like the sound of a storm in a dry forest. All round about the cañon these passing wonderful Snail People made a road (line) of magic medicine and sacred meal, which road, even as a corral, no game animal, even though great Elk or strong Buck Deer, could pass.

Now, it rained many days, and thus the tracks of all these animals tending thither were washed away. Nowhere could the Kâ'-kâ or the children of men, although they hunted day after day over the plains and mountains, on the mesas and along the cañon-valleys, find prey or trace of prey.

Thus it happened that after many days they grew hungry, almost famished. Even the great strong Shá'-la-k'o and the swift Sá-la-mo-pi-a walked zigzag in their trails, from the weakness of hunger. At first the mighty Kâ'-kâ and men alike were compelled to eat the bones they had before cast away, and at last to devour the soles of their moccasins and even the deer-tail ornaments of their dresses for want of the flesh of K'iap-in-á-hâ-i, Game animals.

Still, day after day, though weak and disheartened, men and the Kâ'-kâ sought game in the mountains. At last a great Elk was given liberty. His sides shook with tallow, his dewlap hung like a bag, so fleshy was it, his horns spread out like branches of a dead tree, and his crackling hoofs cut the sands and even the rocks as he ran westward. He circled far off toward the Red River, passed through the Round Valley, and into the northern cañons. The Shá'-la-k'o was out hunting.

He espied the deep tracks of the elk and fleetly followed him. Passing swift and strong was he, though weak from hunger, and ere long he came in sight of the great Elk. The sight gladdened and strengthened him; but alas! the Elk kept his distance as he turned again toward the hiding-place of his brother animals. On and on the Sha'-la-k'o followed him, until he came to the edge of a great cañon, and peering over the brink discovered the hiding-place of all the game animals of the world.

"Aha! so here you all are," said he. "I'll hasten back to my father, Pá-u-ti-wa,* who hungers for flesh, alas! and grows weak." And like the wind the Shá'-la-k'o returned to Kó-thlu-ël-lon-ne. Entering, he informed the Kâ'-kâ, and word was sent out by the swift Sá-la-mo-pi-a† to all the We-ma-á-hâ-i for counsel and assistance, for the We-ma-á-hâ-i were now the Fathers of men and the Kâ'-kâ. The Mountain Lion, the Coyote, the Wild Cat, the Wolf, the Eagle, the Falcon, the Ground Owl, and the Mole were summoned, all hungry and lean, as were the Kâ'-kâ and the children of men, from want of the flesh of the game animals. Nevertheless, they were anxious for the hunt and moved themselves quickly among one another in their anxiety. Then the passing swift runners, the Sá-la-mo-pi-a, of all colors, the yellow, the blue, the red, the white, the many colored, and the black, were summoned to accompany the We-ma-á-hâ-i to the cañon-valley of the Snail People. Well they knew that passing wonderful were the Snail People, and that no easy matter would it be to overcome their medicine and their magic. But they hastened forth until they came near to the cañon. Then the Shá'-la-k'o,‡ who guided them, gave directions that they should make themselves ready for the hunt.

When all were prepared, he opened by his sacred power the magic corral on the northern side, and forth rushed a great buck Deer.

"Long Tail, the corral has been opened for thee. Forth comes thy game, seize him!" With great leaps the Mountain Lion overtook and threw the Deer to the ground, and fastened his teeth in his throat.

The corral was opened on the western side. Forth rushed a Mountain Sheep.

"Coyote, the corral has been opened for thee. Forth comes thy game, seize him!" The Coyote dashed swiftly forward. The Mountain Sheep dodged him and ran off toward the west. The Coyote crazily ran about

* The chief god of the Kâ'-kâ, now represented by masks, and the richest costuming known to the Zuñis, which are worn during the winter ceremonials of the tribe.

† The Sá-la-mo-pi a are monsters with round heads, long snouts, huge feathered necks, and human bodies. They are supposed to live beneath the waters, to come forth or enter snout foremost. They also play an important part in the Kâ'-kâ or sacred dances of winter.

‡ Monster human bird forms, the warrior chiefs of Pá-u-ti-wa, the representatives of which visit Zuñi, from their supposed western homes in certain springs, each New Year. They are more than twelve feet high, and are carried swiftly about by persons concealed under their dresses.

yelping and barking after his game, but the Mountain Sheep bounded from rock to rock and was soon far away. Still the Coyote rushed crazily about, until the Mountain Lion commanded him to be quiet. But the Coyote smelled the blood of the Deer and was beside himself with hunger. Then the Mountain Lion said to him disdainfully, "Satisfy thy hunger on the blood that I have spilled, for to-day thou hast missed thy game; and thus ever will thy descendants like thee blunder in the chase. As thou this day satisfiest thy hunger, so also by the blood that the hunter spills or the flesh that he throws away shall thy descendants forever have being."

The corral was opened on the southern side. An Antelope sprang forth. With bounds less strong than those of the Mountain Lion, but nimbler, the Wild Cat seized him and threw him to the ground.

The corral was opened on the eastern side. Forth ran the Ó-ho-li (or albino antelope). The Wolf seized and threw him. The Jack Rabbit was let out. The Eagle poised himself for a moment, then swooped upon him. The Cotton Tail came forth. The Prey Mole waited in his hole and seized him; the Wood Rat, and the Falcon made him his prey; the Mouse, and the Ground Owl quickly caught him.

While the We-ma-á-hâ-i were thus satisfying their hunger, the game animals began to escape through the breaks in the corral. Forth through the northern door rushed the Buffalo, the great Elk, and the Deer, and toward the north the Mountain Lion, and the yellow Sá-la-mo-pi-a swiftly followed and herded them, to the world where stands the yellow mountain, below the great northern ocean.

Out through the western gap rushed the Mountain Sheep, herded and driven by the Coyote and the blue Sá-la-mo-pi-a, toward the great western ocean, where stands the ancient blue mountain.

Out through the southern gap rushed the Antelope, herded and driven by the Wild Cat and the red Sá-la-mo-pi-a, toward the great land of summer, where stands the ancient red mountain.

Out through the eastern gap rushed the Ó-ho-li, herded and driven by the Wolf and the white Sá-la-mo-pi-a, toward where "they say" is the eastern ocean, the "Ocean of day", wherein stands the ancient white mountain.

Forth rushed in all directions the Jack Rabbit, the Cotton Tail, the Rats, and the Mice, and the Eagle, the Falcon, and the Ground Owl circled high above, toward the great "Sky ocean," above which stands the ancient mountain of many colors, and they drove them over all the earth, that from their homes in the air they could watch them in all places; and the Sá-la-mo-pi-a of many colors rose and assisted them.

Into the earth burrowed the Rabbits, the Rats, and the Mice, from the sight of the Eagle, the Falcon, and the Ground Owl, but the Prey Mole and the black Sá-la-mo-pi-a thither followed them toward the four caverns (wombs) of earth, beneath which stands the ancient black mountain.

Then the earth and winds were filled with rumbling from the feet of the departing animals, and the Snail People saw that their game was escaping; hence the world was filled with the wars of the Kâ'-kâ, the Snail People, and the children of men.

Thus were let loose the game animals of the world. Hence the Buffalo, the Great Elk, and the largest Deer are found mostly in the north, where they are ever pursued by the great Mountain Lion; but with them escaped other animals, and so not alone in the north are the Buffalo, the Great Elk, and the Deer found.

Among the mountains and the cañons of the west are found the Mountain Sheep, pursued by the Coyote; but with them escaped many other animals; hence not alone in the west are the Mountain Sheep found.

Toward the south escaped the Antelopes, pursued by the Wild Cat. Yet with them escaped many other animals; hence not alone in the south are the Antelopes found.

Toward the east escaped the Ó-ho-li, pursued by the Wolf; but with them escaped many other animals; hence not alone in the east are the Ó-ho-li-we found.

Forth in all directions escaped the Jack Rabbits, Cotton Tails, Rats, and Mice; hence over all the earth are they found. Above them in the skies circle the Eagle, the Falcon, and the Ground Owl; yet into the earth escaped many of them, followed by the Prey Mole; hence beneath the earth burrow many.

Thus, also, it came to be that the Yellow Mountain Lion is the master Prey Being of the north, but his younger brothers, the blue, the red, the white, the spotted, and the black Mountain Lions wander over the other regions of earth. Does not the spotted Mountain Lion (evidently the Ocelot) live among the *high* mountains of the south?

Thus, too, was it with the Coyote, who is the master of the West, but whose younger brothers wander over all the regions; and thus, too, with the Wild Cat and the Wolf.

In this tradition there is an attempt, not only to explain the special distribution throughout the six regions, of the Prey animals and their prey, but also to account for the occurrence of animals in regions other than those to which, according to this classification, they properly belong.

THEIR VARIETIES.

We find, therefore, that each one of the six species of Prey animals is again divided into six varieties, according to color, which determines the location of each variety in that one or other of the regions with which its color agrees, yet it is supposed to owe allegiance to its

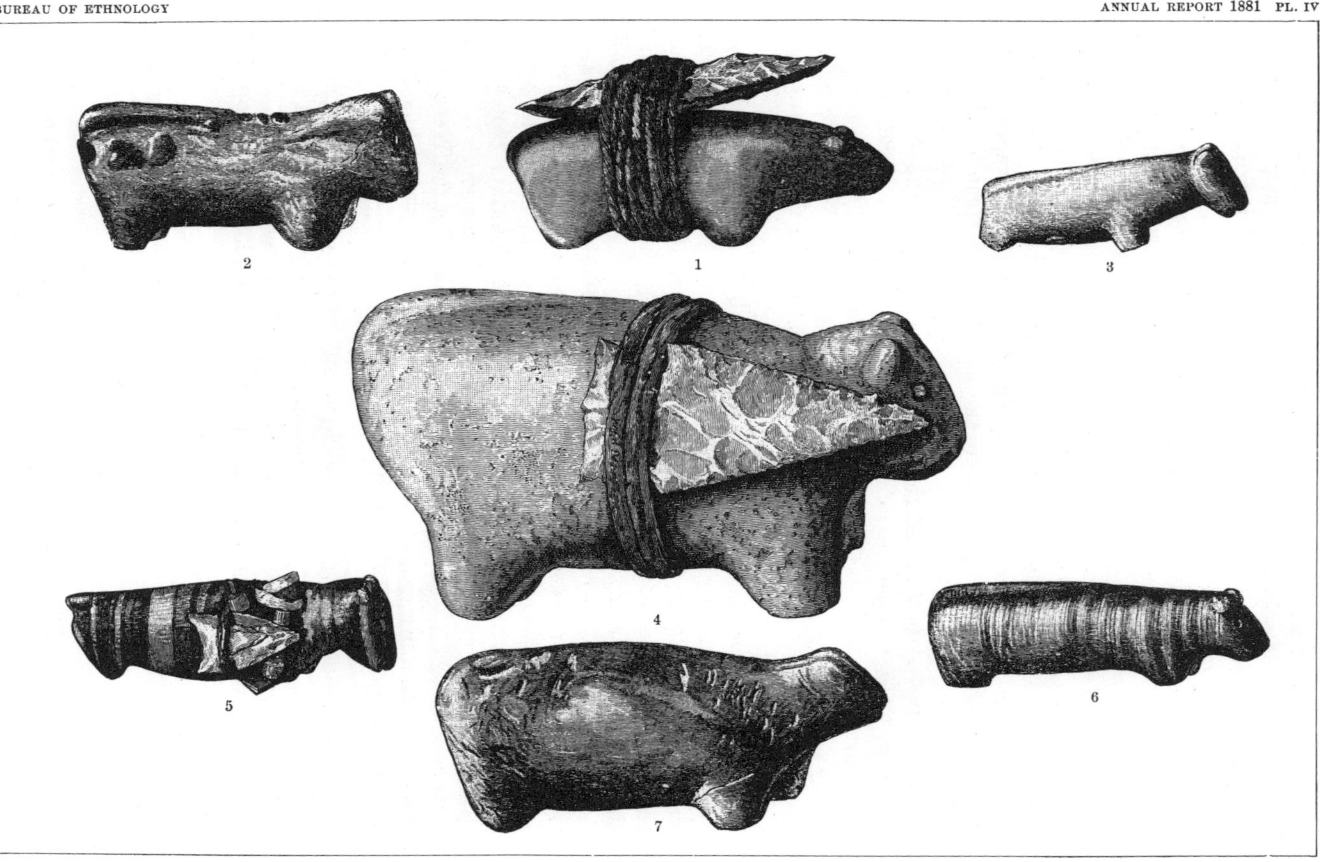

THE MOUNTAIN LION FETICHES OF THE CHASE—HUNTER GOD OF THE NORTH.

representative, whatsoever this may be or wheresoever placed. For instance, the Mountain Lion is primarily god of the North, but he is supposed to have a representative (younger brother) in the West (the blue Mountain Lion), another in the South (the Red), in the East (the White), in the Upper regions (the Spotted), and in the Lower regions (the black Mountain Lion).

Hence, also, there are six varieties of the fetich representing any one of these divisions, the variety being determined by the color, as expressed either by the material of which the fetich is formed, or the pigment with which it is painted, or otherwise, as, for example, by inlaying. (Plate III, Fig. 4, and Plate VII, Fig. 2.)

THE MOUNTAIN LION—HUNTER GOD OF THE NORTH.

According to this classification, which is native, the fetiches of the Mountain Lions are represented on Plate IV. They are invariably distinguished by the tail, which is represented very long, and laid lengthwise of the back from the rump nearly or quite to the shoulders, as well as by the ears, which are quite as uniformly rounded and not prominent.

The fetich of the yellow Mountain Lion (Hâ'k-ti tä'sh-a-na thlúp-tsi-na), or God of the North (Plate IV, Fig. 1), is of yellow limestone.* It has been smoothly carved, and is evidently of great antiquity, as shown by its polish and patina, the latter partly of blood. The anus and eyes are quite marked holes made by drilling. An arrow-point of flint is bound to the back with cordage of cotton, which latter, however, from its newness, seems to have been recently added.

The fetich of the blue Mountain Lion, of the West (Hâ'k-ti tä'sh-a-na thlí-a-na), is represented in Plate IV, Fig. 2. The original is composed of finely veined azurite or carbonate of copper, which, although specked with harder serpentinous nodules, is almost entirely blue. It has been carefully finished, and the ears, eyes, nostrils, mouth, tail, anus, and legs are clearly cut.

The fetich of the white Mountain Lion, of the East (Hâ'k-ti tä'sh-a na k'ó-ha-na), is represented by several specimens, two of which are reproduced in Plate IV, Figs. 3 and 4. The former is very small and composed of compact white limestone, the details being pronounced, and the whole specimen finished with more than usual elaboration. The latter is unusually large, of compact gypsum or alabaster, and quite carefully carved. The eyes have been inlaid with turkoises, and there is cut around its neck a groove by which the beads of shell, coral, &c., were originally fastened. A large arrow-head of chalcedony has been bound with cords of cotton flatwise along one side of the body.

The only fetich representing the red Mountain Lion, of the South (Hâ'k-ti tä'sh-a-na á-ho-na), in the collection was too imperfect for reproduction.

---

* I am indebted to Mr. S. F. Emmons, of the Geological Survey, for assisting me to determine approximately the mineralogical character of these specimens.

The fetich of the spotted or many-colored Mountain Lion (Hâ'k-ti tä'sh-a-na sú-pa-no-pa *or* í-to-pa-nah-na-na), of the Upper regions, is also represented by two specimens (Plate IV, Figs. 5 and 6), both of fibrous aragonite in alternating thin and thick laminæ, or bands of grayish yellow, white, and blue. Fig. 5 is by far the more elaborate of the two, and is, indeed, the most perfect fetich in the collection. The legs, ears, eyes, nostrils, mouth, tail, anus, and genital organs (of the male) are carefully carved, the eyes being further elaborated by mosaics of minute turkoises. To the right side of the body, "over the heart," is bound with blood-blackened cotton cords a delicate flint arrow-point, together with white shell and coral beads, and, at the breast, a small triangular figure of an arrow in haliotus, or abalone.

The fetich of the black Mountain Lion (Hâ'k-ti tä'sh-a-na shí-k'ia-na) (Pl. IV, Fig. 7) is of gypsum, or white limestone, but has been painted black by pigment, traces of which are still lodged on portions of its surface.

THE COYOTE–HUNTER GOD OF THE WEST.

The fetiches of the Coyote, or God of the West, and his younger brothers, represented on Plate V, are called Téthl-po-k'ia, an archaic form of the modern word Sús-k'i wé-ma-we (Coyote fetiches), from *téthl-nan*, = a sacred prayer-plume, and *pó-an*, = an object or locality on or toward which anything is placed, a depository, and *k'ia* = the active participle. They are usually distinguished by horizontal or slightly drooping tails, pointed or small snouts, and erect ears. Although the Coyote of the West is regarded as the master of the Coyotes of the other five regions, yet, in the prayers, songs, and recitations of the Sá-ni-a-k'ia-kwe, and Prey Brother Priesthood, the Coyote of the North is mentioned first. I therefore preserve the same sequence observed in describing the Mountain Lion fetiches.

The fetich of the yellow Coyote (Sús-k'i thlúp-tsi-na), of the North, is represented in Plate V, Fig. 1. The original is of compact white limestone stained yellow. The attitude is that of a coyote about to pursue his prey (lá-hi-na í-mo-na), which has reference to the intemperate haste on the part of this animal, which usually, as in the foregoing tradition, results in failure.

The fetich of the blue Coyote, of the West (Sús-k'i ló-k'ia-na—signifying in reality blue gray, the color of the coyote, instead of blue=thlí-a-na), is shown in Plate V, Fig. 2. This fetich is also of compact white limestone, of a yellowish gray color, although traces of blue paint and large turkois eyes indicate that it was intended, like Plate III, Fig. 3, to represent the God of the West.

The fetich of the red Coyote (Sús-k'i á-ho-na), of the South, is represented by Plate V, Fig. 4, which, although of white semi-translucent calcite, has been deeply stained with red paint.

Two examples of the fetich of the white Coyote (Sús-k'i k'ó-ha-na), of the East, are shown in Plate V, Figs. 4 and 5. They are both of com.

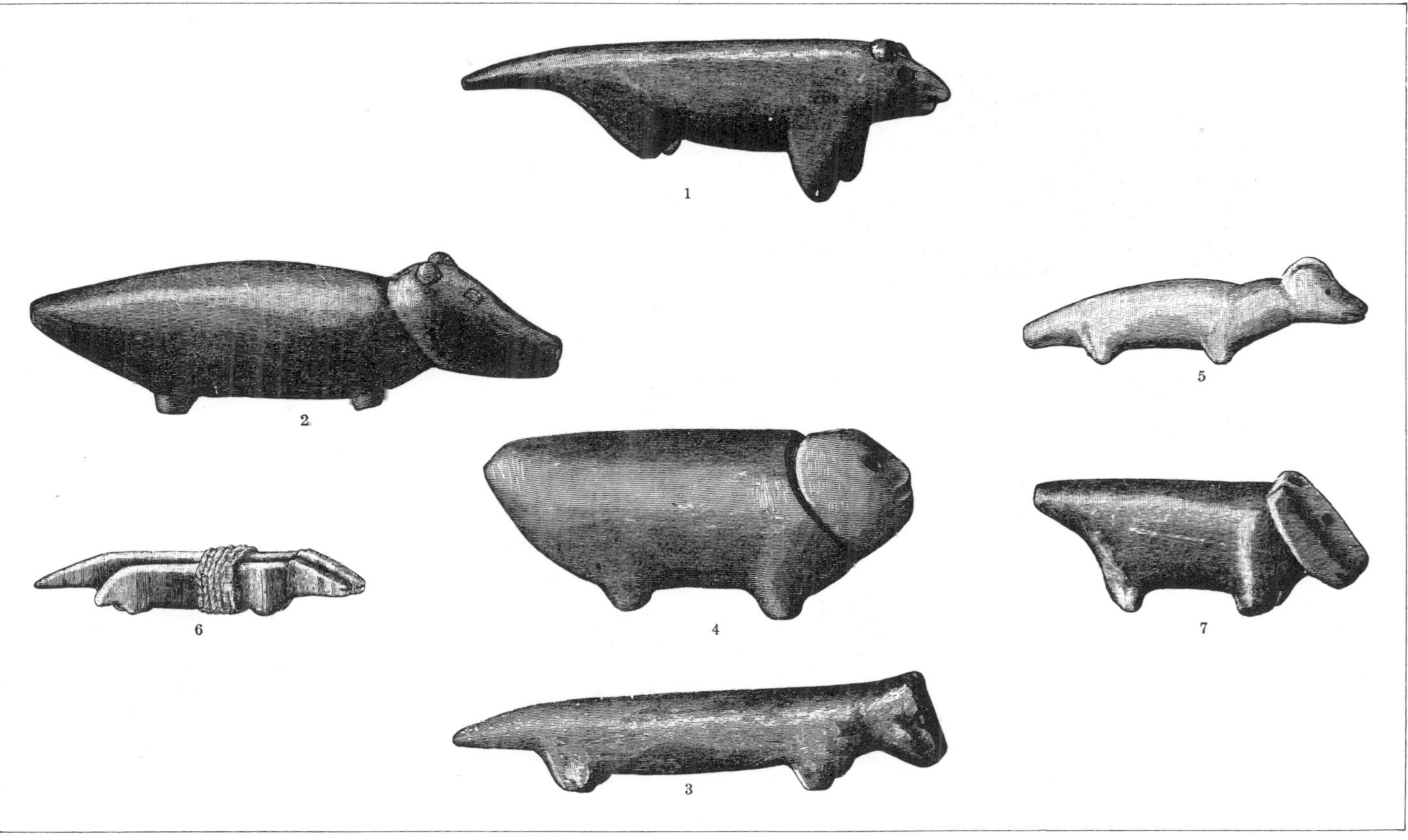

THE COYOTE FETICHES OF THE CHASE—HUNTER GOD OF THE WEST.

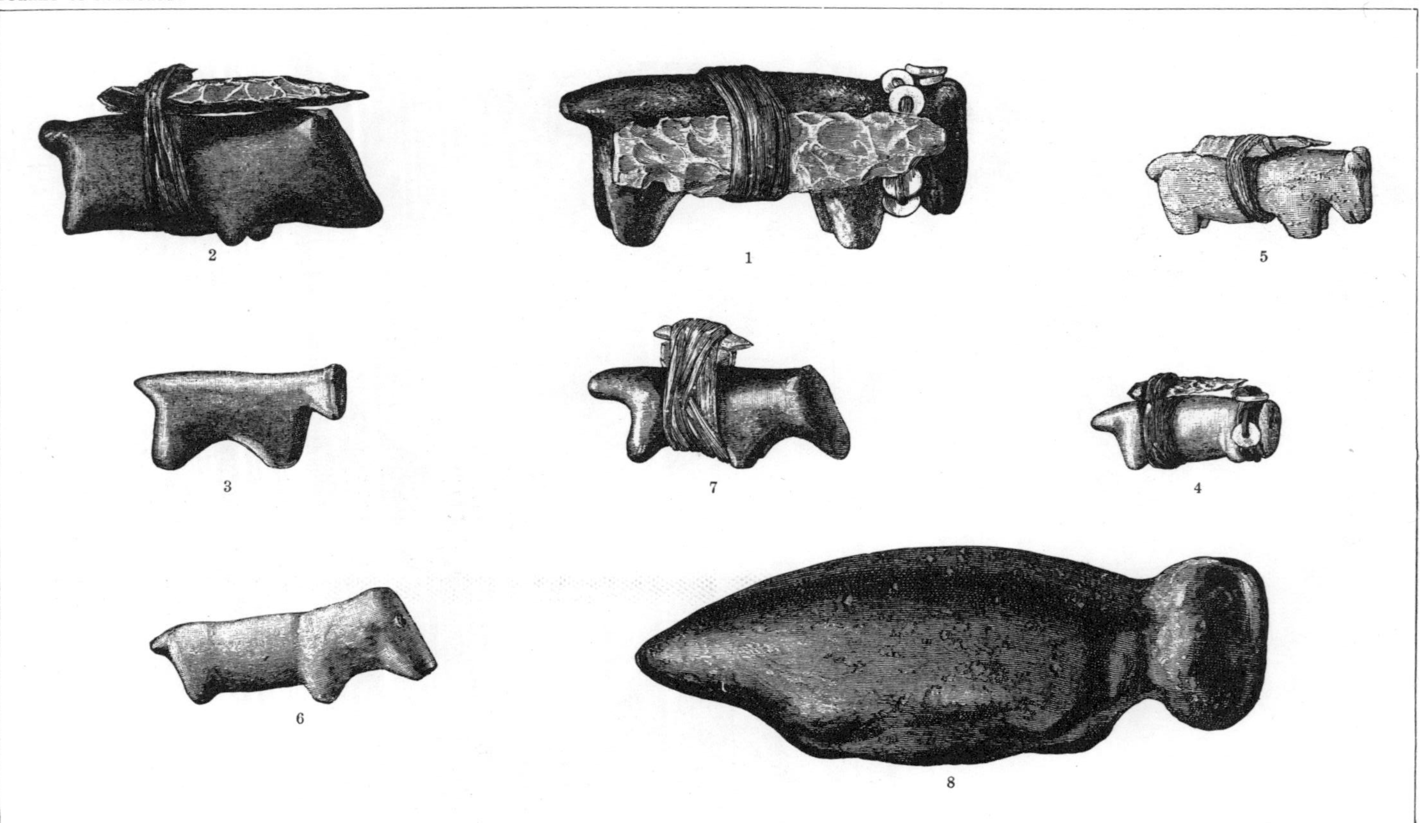

WILD CAT FETICHES OF THE CHASE—HUNTER GOD OF THE SOUTH.

pact white limestone. The first is evidently a natural fragment, the feet being but slightly indicated by grinding, the mouth by a deep cut straight across the snout, and the eyes by deeply drilled depressions, the deep groove around the neck being designed merely to receive the necklace. The second, however, is more elaborate, the pointed chin, horizontal tail, and pricked-up ears being distinctly carved, and yet in form the specimen resembles more a weasel than a coyote.

The fetich of the many-colored Coyote (Sús-k'i í-to-pa-nah-na-na), of the Upper regions, is reproduced in Plate V, Fig. 6, which represents the male and female together, the latter being indicated merely by the smaller size and the shorter tail. They are both of aragonite. This conjoined form of the male and female fetiches is rare, and is significant of other powers than those of the hunt.

The black Coyote (Sús-k'i shí-k'ia-na), of the Lower regions, is represented by Plate V, Fig. 7, the original of which is of compact white limestone or yellowish-gray marble, and shows traces of black paint or staining.

THE WILD-CAT—HUNTER GOD OF THE SOUTH.

The fetiches of the Wild Cat, the principal of which is God of the South, are represented on Plate VI. They are characterized by short horizontal tails and in most cases by vertical faces and short ears, less erect than in the fetiches of the Coyote.

Plate VI, Fig. 1, represents the fetich of the yellow Wild Cat (Té-pi thlúp-tsi-na) of the North. Although of yellow limestone, it is stained nearly black with blood. A long, clearly-chipped arrow-point of chalcedony is bound with blood-stained cotton cordage along the right side of the figure, and a necklace of white shell beads (Kó-ha-kwa), with one of black stone (Kewí-na-kwa) among them, encircles the neck.

Plate VI, Fig. 2, represents the fetich of the blue Wild Cat (Té-pi thlí-a-na), of the West. It is formed from basaltic clay of a grayish-blue color, and is furnished with an arrow-point of jasper (jasp vernis), upon which is laid a small fragment of turkois, both secured to the back of the specimen with sinew taken from the animal represented. Plate VI, Fig. 3, likewise represents the fetich of the Wild Cat of the West. It is a fragment from a thin vein of malachite and azurite, or green and blue carbonate of copper, and has been but little changed from its original condition.

Plate VI, Fig. 4, represents the red Wild Cat (Té-pi á-ho-na), of the South. Although formed from gypsum or yellow limestone, its color has been changed by the application of paint. It is supplied with the usual necklace and arrow-point of the perfect fetich, secured by bands of sinew and cotton.

Both Figs. 5 and 6 of Plate VI represent the fetich of the white Wild Cat (Té-pi k'ó-ha-na), of the East, and are of compact white limestone carefully fashioned and polished, the one to represent the perfect animal, the other the fœtus. This specimen, like Plate V, Fig. 6, has a significance other than that of a mere fetich of the chase, a significance connected with the Phallic worship of the Zuñis, on which subject I hope ere many years to produce interesting evidence.

Plate VI, Fig. 7, represents the fetich of the many-colored Wild Cat (Té-pi sú-pa-no-pa), of the Upper regions, which is made of basaltic clay, stained black with pitch and pigment, and furnished with a flake of flint and a small fragment of chrysocolla, both of which are attached to the back of the figure with a binding of sinew.

Plate VI, Fig. 8, represents, according to the Zuñis, a very ancient and valued fetich of the black Wild Cat (Té-pi shí-k'ia-na), of the Lower regions. It is little more than a concretion of compact basaltic rock, with slight traces of art. Its natural form, however, is suggestive of an animal. Long use has polished its originally black surface to the hue of lustrous jet.

THE WOLF—HUNTER GOD OF THE EAST.

The fetiches of the Wolf, God of the East, and of his younger brothers (Iú-na-wi-ko wé-ma-we) are represented on Plate VII. They are characterized by erect attitudes, usually oblique faces, pricked-up ears, and "hanging tails."

Plate VII, Fig. 1, is a representation of the fetich of the yellow Wolf (Iú-na-wi-ko thlúp-tsi-na), of the North. It is of yellow indurated claystone. In this example the legs are much longer than in most specimens, for nearly all these figures are either natural fragments or concretions slightly improved on by art, or are figures which have been suggested by and derived from such fragments or concretions. Moreover, the ceremonials to be described further on require that they should be "able to stand alone"; therefore they are usually furnished with only rudimentary legs. The tail is only indicated, while in nearly all other Wolf fetiches it is clearly cut down the rump, nearly to the gambol joint.

Plate VII, Fig. 2, represents a fetich of the blue Wolf (Iú-na-wi-ko thlí-a-na), of the West. It is of gray sandstone, stained first red, then blue, the latter color being further indicated by settings of green turkois on either side and along the back, as well as in the eyes.

Plate VII, Fig. 3, represents the fetich of the red Wolf (Iú-na-wi-ko á-ho-na), of the South. It is but crudely formed from a fragment of siliceous limestone, the feet, ears, and tail being represented only by mere protuberances. Although the material is naturally of a yellowish-gray color, it has been stained red.

Plate VII, Fig. 4, represents the fetich of the white Wolf (Iú-na-wi-ko k'ó-ha-na), of the East. It is of very white, compact limestone. The hanging tail, erect ears, attitude, &c., are better shown in this than perhaps in any other specimen of the class in the collection. It has, however, been broken through the body and mended with black pitch.

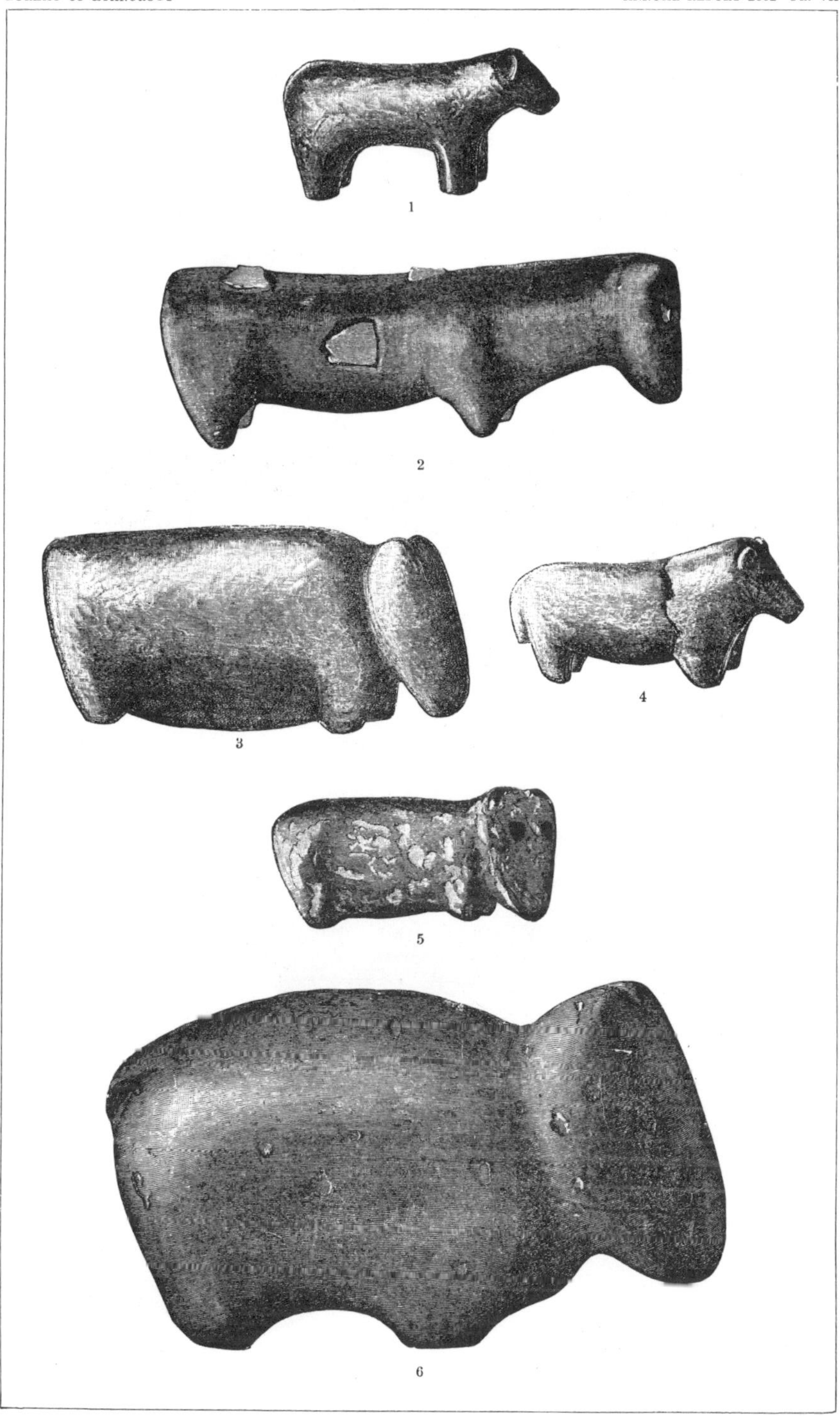

WOLF FETICHES OF THE CHASE—HUNTER GOD OF THE EAST.

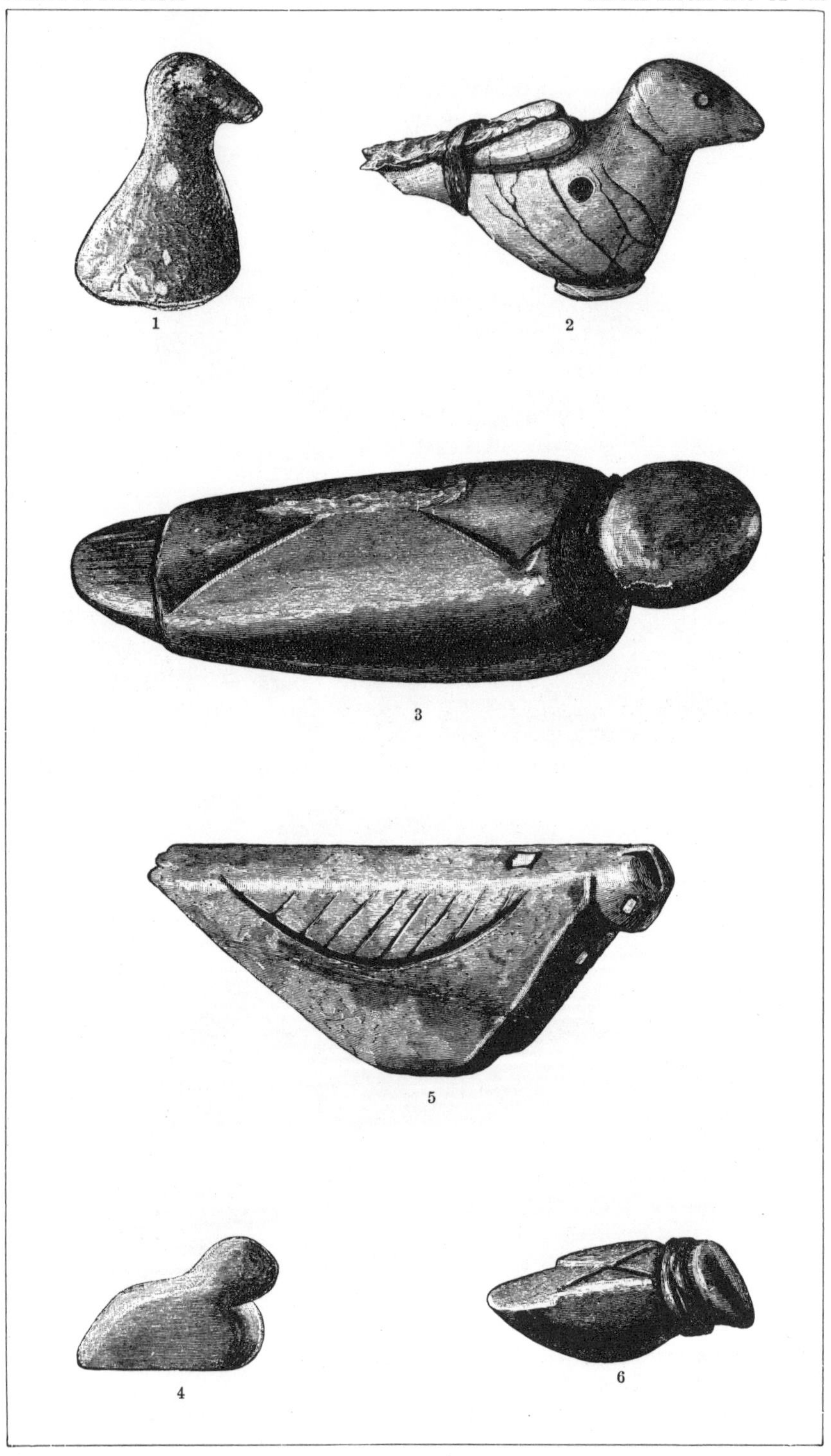

EAGLE FETICHES OF THE CHASE—HUNTER GOD OF THE UPPER REGIONS.

Plate VII, Fig. 5, represents the fetich of the many-colored Wolf (Iú-na-wi-ko í-to-pa-nah-na-na), of the Upper regions. The original is of fine-grained sandstone of a gray color, stained in some places faintly with red and other tints. The mouth, eyes, ear tips, and tail have been touched with black to make them appear more prominent.

Plate VII, Fig. 6, represents the fetich of the black Wolf (Iú-na-wi-ko shí-k'ia-na), of the Lower regions. Although uncommonly large and greatly resembling in form the bear, it possesses the oblique face, upright ears, hanging tail, and other accepted characteristics of the Wolf.

THE EAGLE—HUNTER GOD OF THE UPPER REGIONS.

The fetiches of the Eagle, God of the Upper regions, and his younger brothers of the other regions (K'iä'-k'iä-li wé-ma-we) are represented on Plate VIII. They are characterized merely by rude bird forms, with wings either naturally or very conventionally carved (Figs. 3 and 6). Further details are rarely attempted, from the fact that all the other principal prey animals are quadrupeds, and the simple suggestion of the bird form is sufficient to identify the eagle among any of them.

Plate VIII, Fig. 1, represents the fetich of the yellow Eagle (K'iä'-k'iä-li thlúp-tsi-na), of the Northern skies. It consists merely of the head and shoulders, very rudely formed of white limestone and painted with yellow ocher. This specimen is doubtless a natural fragment very little altered by art.

Plate VIII, Fig. 2, represents the fetich of the blue Eagle (K'iä'-k'iä-li ló-k'ia-na), of the Western skies. It is quite elaborately carved, supplied with a pedestal, and pierced through the body to facilitate suspension. For during ceremonials, to be described further on, the fetiches of the Eagle are usually suspended, although sometimes, like those of the quadrupeds, they are placed on the floor, as indicated by the pedestal furnished to this specimen. Although of compact white limestone, this fetich is made to represent the blue Eagle by means of turkois eyes and a green stain over the body. A small pink chalcedony arrow point is attached to the back between the wings by means of a single sinew band passed around the tips of the latter and the tail and under the wings over the shoulders.

Plate VIII, Fig. 3, represents the fetich of the red Eagle (K'iä'-k'iä-li á-ho-na), of the Southern skies. Like Fig. 42, this is doubtless a nearly natural fragment of very fine-grained red sandstone, the wings being indicated by deep lines which cross over the back, and the rump grooved to receive the cord with which to secure to the back an arrow-point. The breast is perforated.

Plate VIII, Fig. 4, is a nearly natural fragment of compact white limestone, representing the white Eagle (K'iä'-k'iä-li k'ó-ha-na), of the Eastern skies. No artificial details, save the eyes, which are faintly indicated, have been attempted on this specimen.

Plate VIII, Fig. 5, represents, in compact yellow limestone, the speckled

Eagle (K'iä'-k'iä-li sú-tchu-tchon-ne) of the Upper regions, the drab color of the body being varied by fragments of pure turkois inserted into the eyes, breast, and back. A notch in the top and front of the head probably indicates that the specimen was once supplied with a beak, either of turkois or of white shell. It is perforated lengthwise through the breast.

Plate VIII, Fig. 6, is a representation of a thoroughly typical conventional fetich of the black Eagle (K'iä'-k'iä-li kwín-ne) of the Lower regions. It is of calcite, stained lustrous black. A cotton cord around the neck supplies the place of the original "necklace."

THE MOLE—HUNTER GOD OF THE LOWER REGIONS.

The fetiches of the Mole, or God of the Lower regions (K'iä'-lu-tsi wé-ma-we, in the sacred orders; Maí-tu-pu wé-ma-we, in the order of the Hunt), are represented in the collection by only two specimens, Plate II, Fig. 6, and Plate IX, Fig. 1. The figure of a third specimen, taken from one of my sketches of the original in Zuñi, is given on Plate III, Fig. 5.

These fetiches being unpopular, because considered less powerful than those of the larger gods of prey, are very rare, and are either rude concretions with no definite form (Plate II, Fig. 6), or almost equally rude examples of art, as in Plate IX, Fig. 1, which represents the fetich of the white Mole (Maí-tu-pu kó-ha-na) of the Eastern Lower regions. It consists merely of a natural slab of fine white limestone.

Nevertheless, value is sometimes attached to the Mole, from the fact that it is able by burrowing to lay traps for the largest game of earth, which it is supposed to do consciously. For this reason it is sometimes represented with surprising fidelity, as in Plate III, Fig. 5.

THE GROUND OWL AND THE FALCON.

The fetiches of the Ground Owl (the Prairie Dog variety—Thlá-po-po-ke'-a' wé-ma-we) of all regions, are still more rarely represented and even less prized than those of the Mole. The only example in the collection is reproduced in Plate IX, Fig. 2. The original is quite carefully formed of soft white limestone, and is perforated to facilitate suspension.

The Falcon fetiches (Pí-pi wé-ma-we) are included in the Eagle species, as they are called the younger brothers of the Eagle, and supply the place of the red Eagle which variety is met with very rarely.

THEIR RELATIVE VALUES.

The relative value of these varieties of fetiches depends largely upon the rank of the Animal god they represent. For instance, the Mountain Lion is not only master of the North, which takes precedence over

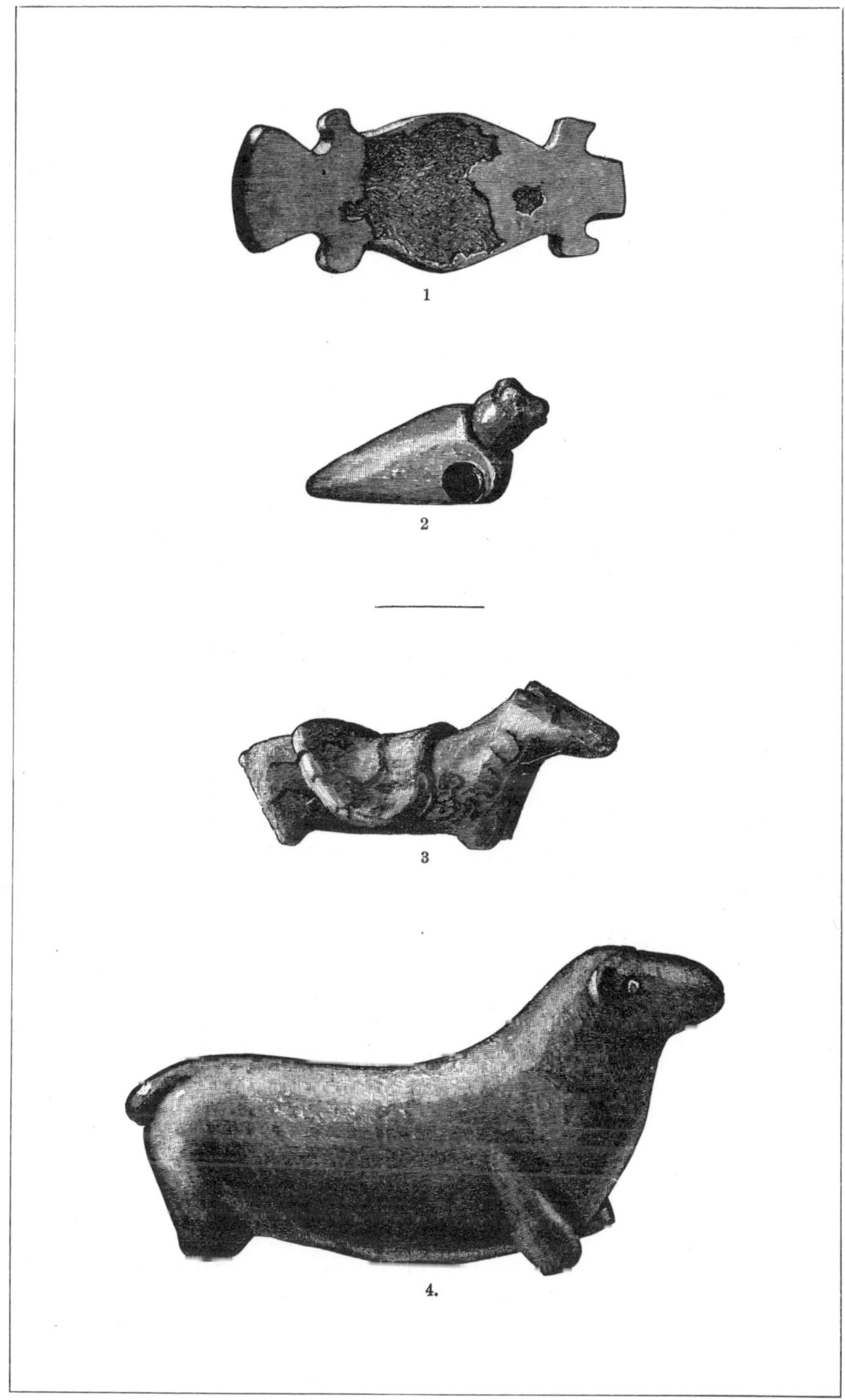

THE MOLE AND THE GROUND-OWL FETICHES—HUNTER GODS OF THE LOWER REGIONS AND ALL REGIONS.

THE NAVAJO FETICHES—PHALLIC GODS OF THE FLOCKS.

all the other "ancient sacred spaces" (Té-thlä-shi-na-we) or regions, but is also the master of all the other Prey gods, if not of all other terrestrial animals. Notwithstanding the fact that the Coyote, in the Order of the Hunt (the Coyote society or the Sá-ni-a-k'ia-kwe), is given for traditional reasons higher *sacred* rank than the Mountain Lion, he is, as a Prey Being, one degree lower, being god of the West, which follows the North in order of importance. Hence we find the Mountain Lion and Coyote fetiches far more prized than any of the others, and correspondingly more numerous. The Coyote in rank is younger brother of the Mountain Lion, just as the Wild Cat is younger brother of the Coyote, the Wolf of the Wild Cat, and so on to the Mole, and less important Ground Owl. In relationship by blood, however, the yellow Mountain Lion is accounted older brother of the blue, red, white, spotted, and black Mountain Lions; the blue Coyote, older brother of the red, white, yellow, mottled or spotted, and black Coyotes. So the Wild Cat of the South is regarded as the older brother of the Wild Cats of all the other five regions. And thus it is respectively with the Wolf, the Eagle, and the Mole. We find, therefore, that in the North all the gods of Prey are represented, as well as the Mountain Lion, only they are yellow. In the West all are represented, as well as the Coyote, only they are blue; and thus throughout the remaining four regions.

The Mountain Lion is further believed to be the special hunter of the Elk, Deer, and Bison (no longer an inhabitant of New Mexico). His fetich is, therefore, preferred by the hunter of these animals. So, also, is the fetich of the Coyote preferred by the hunter of the Mountain Sheep; that of the Wild Cat, by the hunter of the Antelope; that of the Wolf, by the hunter of the rare and highly-valued Ó-ho-li; those of the Eagle and Falcon, by the hunter of Rabbits; and that of the Mole, by the huntĕr of other small game.

The exception to this rule is individual, and founded upon the belief that any one of the gods of Prey hunts to some extent the special game of all the other gods of Prey. Hence, any person who may discover either a concretion or natural object or an ancient fetich calling to mind or representing any one of the Prey gods will regard it as his special fetich, and almost invariably prefer it, since he believes it to have been "meted to" him (añ-ik-tchi-a-k'ia) by the gods.

THEIR CUSTODIAN.

Although these fetiches are thus often individual property, members of the Sá-ni-a-k'ia-kwe, and of the Eagle and Coyote gentes, as well as priests included in the Prey God Brotherhood, are required to deposit their fetiches, when not in use, with the "Keeper of the Medicine of the Deer" (Nál-e-ton í-lo-na), who is usually, if not always, the head member of the Eagle gens.

It rests with these memberships and these alone to perfect the fetiches when found, and to carry on at stated intervals the ceremonials and worship connected with them.

When not in use, either for such ceremonials or for the hunt, these tribal fetiches are kept in a very ancient vessel of wicker-work, in the House of the Deer Medicine (Nál-e-ton ín-kwïn), which is usually the dwelling place of the keeper.

THE RITES OF THEIR WORSHIP.

THE DAY OF THE COUNCIL OF THE FETICHES.

The principal ceremonial connected with the worship of the Prey Beings takes place either a little before or after the winter solstice or national New Year.

This is due to the fact that many of the members of the above-mentioned associations also belong to other societies, and are required on the exact night of the New Year to perform other religious duties than those connected with the fetich worship. Hence, the fetiches or gods of prey have their special New Year's day, called Wé-ma-a-wa ú-pu-k'ia té-wa-ne ("The day of the council of the fetiches").

On this occasion is held the grand council of the fetiches. They are all taken from their place of deposit and arranged, according to species and color, in front of a symbolic slat altar on the floor of the council chamber in a way I have attempted to indicate, as far as possible, by the arrangement of the figures on the plates, the quadrupeds being placed upright, while the Eagles and other winged fetiches are suspended from the rafters by means of cotton cords. Busily engaged in observing other ceremonials and debarred from actual entrance, until my recent initiation into the Priesthood of the Bow, I have unfortunately never witnessed any part of this ceremonial save by stealth, and cannot describe it as a whole. I reserve the right, therefore, to correct any details of the following at some future day.

The ceremonials last throughout the latter two thirds of a night. Each member on entering approaches the altar, and with prayer-meal in hand addresses a long prayer to the assembly of fetiches, at the close of which he scatters the prayer-meal over them, breathes on and from his hand, and takes his place in the council. An opening prayer-chant, lasting from one to three hours, is then sung at intervals, in which various members dance to the sound of the constant rattles, imitating at the close of each stanza the cries of the beasts represented by the fetiches.

At the conclusion of the song, the "Keeper of the Deer Medicine," who is master priest of the occasion, leads off in the recitation of a long metrical ritual, in which he is followed by the two warrior priests with shorter recitations, and by a prayer from another priest (of uncertain rank). During these recitations, responses like those of the litany in the Church of England may be heard from the whole assembly, and at their close, at or after sunrise, all members flock around the altar and repeat, prayer-meal in hand, a concluding invocation. This is followed by a liberal feast, principally of game, which is brought in and served by the women, with additional recitations and ceremonials. At this feast, portions of each kind of food are taken out by every member for the Prey gods, which portions are sacrificed by the priests, together with the prayer plume-sticks, several of which are supplied by each member.

CEREMONIALS OF THE HUNT.

Similar midnight ceremonials, but briefer, are observed on the occasion of the great midwinter tribal hunts, the times for which are fixed by the Keeper of the Deer Medicine, the master and warrior priests of the Sá-ni-a-k'ia-kwe; and the religious observances accompanying and following which would form one of the most interesting chapters connected with the fetich worship of the Zuñis.

These ceremonials and tribal hunts are more and more rarely observed, on account of the scarcity of game and of the death a few years since of the warrior priest above mentioned, without whose assistance they cannot be performed. This position has been recently refilled, and I hope during the coming winter to be enabled, not only to witness one of these observances, but also to join in it; a privilege which will be granted to me on account of my membership in the order of the Priesthood of the Bow.

Any hunter, provided he be one privileged to participate in the above described ceremonials—namely, a Prey brother—supplies himself, when preparing for the chase, not only with his weapons, &c., but also with a favorite or appropriate prey fetich. In order to procure the latter he proceeds, sooner or later before starting, to the House of the Deer Medicine (Nál-e-ton ï'n-kwïn), where the vessel containing the fetiches is brought forth by the Keeper or some substitute, and placed before him. Facing in the direction of the region to which belongs the particular fetich which he designs to use, he sprinkles into and over the vessel sacred prayer or medicine meal. Then holding a small quantity of the meal in his left hand, over the region of his heart, he removes his head-band and utters the following prayer:

Ma:	Lú-k'ia	yät-ton-né,	hom	tä-tchú,	hom	tsi-tá,	tom	lithl	hâ	té-
Why!	This	day,	my	father,	my	mother,	(to) thee	here	I	un-

kwïn-te	té-ä-tip,	o-ná	ël-le-te-k'iá.	Hothl	yam	á-tä-tchú	Kâ-kâ	A'-shi-
expectedly	have	trail (by) road	overtaken.	Soever	for my	Fathers	sacred dance	priest-

wa-ní,	wé-ma	á-shi-wa-ní,	K'ia-pin-a-hâ-í	awën	hâ	lithl	yam
(gods),	Prey	priest-(gods),	the animal gods beings	theirs	I	here	my for them

te-li-ki-ná	yel-le-te-u-k'o-ná	te-li-ki-ná	i-thle-a-nán	tom	lithl	hâ	o-ná
sacred things (plumes, etc., literally relatives of the species.)	made ready	(which) sacred things	with (me) bringing	unto thee	here	I	road by trail

ël-le-te-k'iá; tom lithl hâ häl-lo-wa-ti-nán thle-a-ú tom an té-ap-k'o-nan
overtaken (have); unto thee here I good fortune (ad)dress thy own wherewith (thou hast being)

ä'n-ti-shem-án a-k'iá yam á-wi-te-lin tsi-tá, hâ lithl té-u-su a-k'iá
wishing for hence, to my all earth mother I here (with prayer) (-from), prayer hence,

ó-ne yäthl kwai-k'ia-ná.
trail over go out shall.

Lé-we ú-lokh nan thla-ná tom te-ap-k'o-nán sho-hi-tá tom pi-nan
Thus much (of the) world great thy wherewith (thou hast being) (the) deer thy wind breath (of life)

a-k'iá a-u-la-shó. Awen shi-nán, awen k'iáh-kwïn hothl án-ti-she-mán
by hence encircle about wander around. Their flesh their Life fluid (blood) soever wanting

a-k'iá le-hok té-u-su a k'iá hâ ó-ne yäthl kwaí k'ia-ná.
hence yonder (from me) prayer hence with I trail over go out (shall).

Kwa-í-no-ti-nam hothl yam té-ap-k'o-nán a-k'iá hom tâ ke-tsä-ti-
Without fail (unfailingly) wheresoever thy for me wherewith (thou hast being) hence (by) to me thou happy

k'ia-ná. Hom tâ té-k'o-ha-ná an-ík tchi-a-tú.
(make, do). Unto me thou (the) light meet with (*do*).

FREE TRANSLATION.

Why (of course)—

This day, my father (or, my mother), here I, (as if) unexpectedly, meet thee with whatsoever I have made ready of the sacred things of my fathers, the priest gods of the sacred dances, the priest gods of the Prey (beings). These sacred things bringing I have here overtaken thee, and with their good fortune I here address thee. Wishing for that whereby thou hast being, I shall go forth from here prayerfully upon the trails of my earth-mother.

Throughout the whole of this great country, they whereby thou hast being, the deer, by the command of thy wind of life (breath), wander about. It is wishing for their flesh and blood that I shall go forth yonder prayerfully out over the trails.

Let it be without fail that thou shall make me happy with that whereby thou hast being. Grant unto me the light of thy favor.

Then scattering forth the prayer-meal in the direction he proposes to take on the hunt, he chooses from the vessel the fetich, and pressing it to or toward his lips breaths from it and exclaims:

Ha! é-lah-kwá, hom tä-tchú (hom tsi-tá), lú-k'ia yät-ton-né o-né
Ah! Thanks, my father, (my mother), this day trails

yäthl ëh-kwé ta-pan hâ té-u-su a-k'iá, o-né yäthl kwaí-k'ia-ná.
over ahead taking I prayer with trails over go out shall.

FREE TRANSLATION.

Ah! Thanks, my father (or, my mother), this day I shall follow (thee) forth over the trails. Prayerfully over the trails I shall go out.

Should a party be going to the hunt together, all repair to the House of the Deer Medicine, repeating, one by one, the above prayers and ceremonial as the fetiches are drawn.

The fetich is then placed in a little crescent-shaped bag of buckskin which the hunter wears suspended over the left breast (or heart) by a buckskin thong, which is tied above the right shoulder. With it he returns home, where he hangs it up in his room and awaits a favorable rain or snow storm, meanwhile, if but a few days elapse, retaining the fetich in his own house. If a hunter be not a member of the orders above mentioned, while he must ask a member to secure a fetich for him, in the manner described, still he is quite as privileged to use it as is the member himself, although his chances for success are not supposed to be so good as those of the proper owner.

During his journey out the hunter picks from the heart of the *yucca*, or Spanish bayonet, a few thin leaves, and, on reaching the point where an animal which he wishes to capture has rested, or whence it has newly taken flight, he deposits, together with sacrifices hereinafter to be mentioned, a spider knot (hó-tsa-na mu kwí-ton-ne), made of four strands of these yucca leaves. This knot must be tied like the ordinary cat-knot, but invariably from right to left, so that the ends of the four strands shall spread out from the center as the legs of a spider from its body. The knot is further characterized by being tied quite awkwardly, as if by a mere child. It is deposited on the spot over which the heart of the animal is supposed to have rested or passed. Then a forked twig of cedar is cut and stuck very obliquely into the ground, so that the prongs stand in a direction opposite to that of the course taken by the animal, and immediately in front, as it were, of the fore part of its heart, which is represented as entangled in the knot.

This process, in conjunction with the roar of the animal, which the fetich represents, and which is imitated by the hunter on the conclusion of these various ceremonials, is supposed to limit the power of flight of the animal sought, to confine him within a narrow circle, and, together with an additional ceremonial which is invariably performed, even without the other, is supposed to render it a sure prey. This is performed only after the track has been followed until either the animal is in sight, or a place is discovered where it has lain down. Then, in exactly the spot over which the heart of the animal is supposed to have rested, he deposits a sacrifice of corn pollen (tâ-ón-ia), sacred black war paint (tsú-ha-pa)—a kind of plumbago, containing shining particles, and procured by barter from the Ha-va-su-paí (Coçoninos), and from sacred mines toward the west—and prayer or sacred meal, made from white seed-corn (emblematic of terrestrial life or of the foods of mankind), fragments of shell, sand from the ocean, and sometimes turkois or green-stone, ground very fine, and invariably carried in pouches by all members of the sacred societies of Zuñi. To this mixture sacred shell beads or coral are sometimes added. Then, taking out the fetich, he breathes on it and from it, and exclaims "Si!", which signifies "the time has come," or that everything is in readiness. The exact meaning may, perhaps, be made clearer by an example. When all preparations have been made complete for a ceremonial, the word "Si!", uttered by the master priest of the occasion, is a signal for the commencement of the ceremonials. It is therefore substituted for "Ma!", used in the foregoing prayer, whenever any preparations, like sacrifices and ceremonials, precede the prayer.

With this introduction he utters the accompanying prayer:

Lú-k'ia yät ton-né, hom tä-tchú k'ia-pin hâ-í, to-pin-té yät-ton-né, to-
This day my father game raw being, one day

pin-té teh-thli-na-né, tom an o-né yäthl u-lap-nap-té. Hothl yam á-wi-
one night thy own trail over round about (even) though. However to me your earth

te-lin tsi-tau-án to-pin-té i-te-tchu-ná hom tâ an-k'o-ha-ti-ná. Tom an
mother (with) one step to me thou shalt grant (favor). Thy own

k'iah-kwïn an-ti-shi-ma-ná, tom an shi-i-nán án-ti-shi-mán a-k'iá tom
blood life-fluid wanting, thy own flesh wanting, hence to thee,

lithl hâ häl-lo-wa-ti-nán á-thle-a-ú thlâ á-thle-a-ú. Lé-we tá-kuthl po-ti'
here I good fortunes (ad)dress, treasure (ad)dress. Thus much all the woods round about filled

hom an tom yä't-ti-na tsú-ma-k'ie-ná. Hom á-tä-tchú, hom ton án-k'o-
to me mine you grasping strong shall. My all-fathers, to me you favor

ha-ti-na-wá. Hom ton té-k'o-ha-na án-ik-tchi-a-nap-tú.
do (all). To me you light (favor) meet with *do*.

FREE TRANSLATION.

Si! This day, my father, thou game animal, even though thy trail one day and one night hast (been made) round about; however, grant unto me one step of my earth-mother. Wanting thy life-blood, wanting thy flesh, hence I here address to thee good fortune, address to thee treasure.

All ye woods that fill (the country) round about me, (do) grasp for me strongly. [This expression beseeches that the logs, sticks, branches, brambles, and vines shall impede the progress of the chased animal.] My fathers, favor me. Grant unto me the light of your favor, do.

The hunter then takes out his fetich, places its nostrils near his lips, breaths deeply from them, as though to inhale the supposed magic breath of the God of Prey, and puffs long and quite loudly in the general direction whither the tracks tend. He then utters three or four times a long low cry of, "Hu-u-u-u!" It is supposed that the breath of the god, breathed in temporarily by the hunter, and breathed outward toward the heart of the pursued animal, will overcome the latter and stiffen his limbs, so that he will fall an easy prey; and that the low roar, as of the beast of prey, will enter his consciousness and frighten him so as to conceal from him the knowledge of any approach.

The hunter then rises, replaces his fetich, and pursues the trail with all possible ardor, until he either strikes the animal down by means of his weapons, or so worries it by long-continued chase that it becomes an easy capture. Before the "breath of life" has left the fallen deer (if it be such), he places its fore feet back of its horns and, grasping its mouth, holds it firmly closed, while he applies his lips to its nostrils and breathes as much wind into them as possible, again inhaling from the lungs of the dying animal into his own. Then letting go he exclaims:

Ha! é-lah-kwá! hom tä-tchú, hom tcha-lé. Hom tâ tâ-sho-na-né,
Ah! Thanks! my father, my child. To me thou seeds (of earth)
k'iä-she-ma án-ik-tchi-a-nap-tú. Hom tâ té-k'o-ha-na, o-né, yäthl k'ok-
water (want) meet (grant) do. To me thou light trail (favor) over good
shi, án-ik-tchi-a-nap-tú.
meet (grant) do.

FREE TRANSLATION.

Ah! Thanks, my father, my child. Grant unto me the seeds of earth ("daily bread") and the gift of water. Grant unto me the light of thy favor, do.

As soon as the animal is dead he lays open its viscera, cuts through the diaphragm, and makes an incision in the aorta, or in the sac which incloses the heart. He then takes out the prey fetich, breathes on it, and addresses it thus:

Si! Hom tä-tchú, lú-k'ia yät-ton-né, lithl k'ia-pin-hâ-i an k'iáh-kwïn
Si! My father this day here Game animal its life-fluid (blood)
a-k'iá tâs í-k'iah-kwi-ná, tâs i'-ke-i-nan a-k'iá i'-te-li-a-u-ná:
hence with, thou shalt dampen thyself, thou shalt (thy) heart hence with add unto:

FREE TRANSLATION.

Si! My father, this day of the blood of a game being thou shalt drink (water thyself). With it thou shalt enlarge (add unto) thy heart:

He then dips the fetich into the blood which the sac still contains, continuing meanwhile the prayer, as follows:

——— les-tik-lé-a ak'n' hâ-i', k'ia-pin-hâ-i an k'iáh-kwïn, an shí-i-nan
likewise cooked done being, game being raw its fluid (of life) its flesh
a-k'iá hâ's lithl yam í-ke-i-nan í-te-li-a-u-ná.
hence with I shall here my heart add unto (enlarge).

FREE TRANSLATION.

——— likewise, I, a "done" being, with the blood, the flesh of a raw being (game animal), shall enlarge (add unto) my heart.

Which finished, he scoops up, with his hand, some of the blood and sips it; then, tearing forth the liver, ravenously devours a part of it, and exclaims, "É-lah-kwá!" (Thanks).

While skinning and quartering the game he takes care to cut out the *tragus* or little inner lobe of its ear, the clot of blood within the heart (ä'-te mul ú-li-k'o-na), and to preserve some of the hair. Before leaving, he forms of these and of the black paint, corn pollen, beads of turkois or turkois dust, and sacred shell or broken shell and coral beads before mentioned, a ball, and on the spot where the animal ceased to breathe he digs a grave, as it were, and deposits therein, with prayer-meal, this strange mixture, meanwhile saying the following prayer:

Si! Lú-k'ia yät-ton-né, k'ia-pin-hâ-í, tó-pin-ta yät-ton-né tó-pin-ta
Si! This day game being, raw one day, one

teh-thli-na-né, lé-we tom o-né yäthl ú-lap-na-k'ia tap-té lú-k'ia yät-ton-né
night, thus much thy trail over circled about though (even) this day

te-kwïn-té te-ä-ti-pá, tom lithl hâ an-ah-ú'-thla-k'iá. Tom lithl hâ hä'l-lo-
(as if) unexpectedly was it thou here I upward pulling embraced. To thee here, I good

a-ti-nán thle-a-ú. Tom lithl hâ ó-ne-an thle-a-ú. Tom lithl hâ thlâ
fortune address To thee here I corn pollen the yellow address. To thee here I treasure

thle-a-ú. Yam an-i-kwan-a-k'iá hä'l-lo-wa-ti-nan, ó-ne-an, thlâ í-thle-a-u-
address. By thy knowledge-hence good fortune, the yellow, treasure, (thyself) shall

ná tâ thli-mon hâ-i í-ya-k'ia-nan hom an té u-su-pé-nan a-k'iá tâ
dress thou new being (thyself) making shall be my own prayer-speech hence with, thou

yä'-shu-a i-tú loh k'ia-ná. K'ia-pin-á-hâ-i á-te-kwi a-k'iá. Kwa hom
conversing come and go (shall). Game beings raw animals relative to in the direction of with. Not mine

i'-no-ti-nam tun a-k'iá tom lithl hâ hä'l-lo-wa-ti-nan, ó-ne-an, thlâ, á-thle-
fail to hence, to thee here I good fortune, the yellow, treasure (have) all

a-k'iá. Hom tâ té-k'o-ha-na an'-ik-tchi-a-nap-tú. O-né yäthl k'ok-shi
addressed. To me thou light grant (meet) do. Trail over good

hom tâ tcháw' il-lü'p ó-na yá-k'ia-nap-tú.
to me thou children together with, trail finish, *do.*

FREE TRANSLATION.

Si! This day, game animal, even though, for a day and a night, thy trail above (the earth) circled about—this day it has come to pass that I have embraced thee upward (from it). To thee here I address good fortune. To thee here I address the (sacred) pollen. To thee here I address treasure. By thy (magic) knowledge dressing thyself with this good fortune, with this yellow, with this treasure, do thou, in becoming a new being, converse with (or, of) my prayer as you wander to and fro.

That I may become unfailing toward the Game animals all, I have here addressed unto thee good fortune, the yellow and treasure.

Grant unto me the light of thy favor.

Grant unto me a good (journey) over the trail of life, and, together with children, make the road of my existence, do.

During the performance of these ceremonials the fetich is usually placed in a convenient spot to dry, and at their conclusion, with a blessing, it is replaced in the pouch. The hunter either seeks further for game, or, making a pack of his game in its own skin by tying the legs together and crossing them over his forehead like a burden strap, returns home and deposits it either at the door or just within. The women then come, and, breathing from the nostrils, take the dead animal to the center of the room, where, placing its head toward the East, they lay on either side of its body next to the heart an ear of corn (significant of renewed life), and say prayers, which, though short, are not less interesting and illustrative of the subject than those already given, but which, unfortunately, I cannot produce word for word.

The fetich is returned to the Keeper of the Deer Medicine with thanksgiving and a prayer, not unlike that uttered on taking it forth, but which also I am unable to reproduce. It contains a sentence consigning the fetich to its house with its relatives, speaking of its quenched thirst, satisfied hunger, and the prospects of future conquests, etc.

THEIR POWER.

It is believed that without recourse to these fetiches or to prayers and other inducements toward the game animals, especially the deer tribe, it would be useless to attempt the chase. Untrammeled by the Medicine of the Deer, the powers of the fetiches, or the animals of prey represented, the larger game is unconquerable; and no man, however great his endurance, is accounted able to overtake or to weary them. It thus happens that few hunters venture forth without a fetich, even though they belong to none of the memberships heretofore mentioned. Indeed, the wearing of these fetiches becomes almost as universal as is the wearing of amulets and "Medicines" among other nations and Indian tribes; since they are supposed to bring to their rightful possessors or holders, not only success in the chase and in war (in the case of the Warriors or Priests of the Bow), but also good fortune in other matters.

The successful hunter is typical of possession, since the products of his chase yield him food, apparel, ornament, and distinction. It is therefore argued with strange logic that, even though one may not be a hunter, there must exist a connection between the possessions of the hunter and the possessions of that one, and that principally through the fetiches. A man therefore counts it the greatest of good fortune when he happens to find either a natural or artificial object resembling one of the animals of prey. He presents it to a proper member of the Prey Brotherhood, together with the appropriate flint arrow-point and the desirable amount of ornaments (thlâ-â) for dressing (thlé-a-k'ia-na) and finishing (í-ya-k'ia-na), as soon as possible.

PREY GODS OF THE PRIESTHOOD OF THE BOW.

THE KNIFE-FEATHERED MONSTER, THE MOUNTAIN LION, AND THE GREAT WHITE BEAR.

The Priesthood of the Bow possesses three fetiches, two of which are of the We-ma-á-hâ-i, (Plate X, Fig. 2, and Plate XI, Fig. 2.) The other is sometimes classed with these, sometimes with the higher beings, and may be safely said to form a connecting link between the idolatry proper of the Zuñis and their fetichism. These three beings are, the Mountain Lion (Plate X, Fig. 2), the great White Bear (Plate XI, Fig. 2), (Áiŋ-shi k'ó-ha-na—the god of the scalp-taking ceremonials), and the Knife-feathered Monster (Á-tchi-a lä-to-pa), (Plate X, Fig. 1).

This curious god is the hero of hundreds of folklore tales, and the tutelar deity of several of the societies of Zuñi. He is represented as possessing a human form, furnished with flint knife-feathered pinions, and tail. His dress consists of the conventional terraced cap (representative of his dwelling-place among the clouds), and the ornaments, badge, and garments of the Kâ'-kâ. His weapons are the Great Flint-Knife of War, the Bow of the Skies (the Rain-bow), and the Arrow of Lightning, and his guardians or warriors are the Great Mountain Lion of the North and that of the Upper regions.

He was doubtless the original War God of the Zuñis, although now secondary, in the order of war, to the two children of the Sun mentioned at the outset.

Anciently he was inimical to man, stealing and carrying away to his city in the skies the women of all nations, until subdued by other gods and men of magic powers. At present he is friendly to them, rather in the sense of an animal whose food temporarily satisfies him than in the beneficent character of most of the gods of Zuñi.

Both the Great White Bear and the Mountain Lion of the War Priesthood are, as well as the Knife-feathered Demon, beings of the skies. For this reason the fetich of the Mountain Lion of the skies (of aragonite) is preferred by a Priest of the Bow above all other kinds or colors. Unfortunately, none of the fetiches of this priesthood are to be found in the collections of the Bureau, and but one, with its pouch, has been reproduced from the original, which is in my possession. It was not presented to me with my other paraphernalia on the night of the final ceremonials of my initiation into the Priesthood of the Bow, but some months afterward when I was about to start on a dangerous expedition. At this time I was charged with carefully preserving it during life as my special fetich, and instructed in the various usages connected with

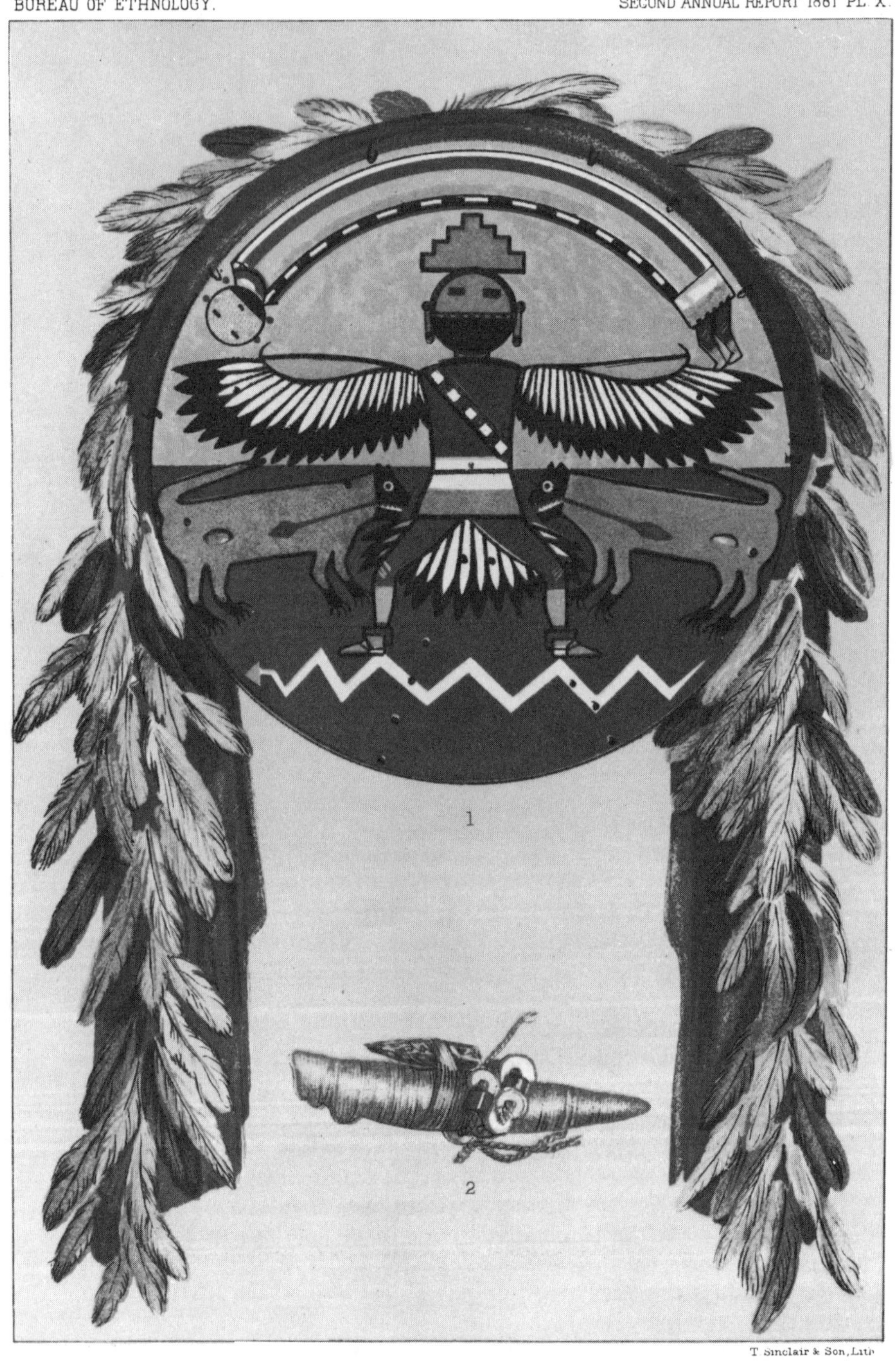

T. Sinclair & Son, Lith.

SHIELD AND FETICH OF THE PRIESTHOOD OF THE BOW.

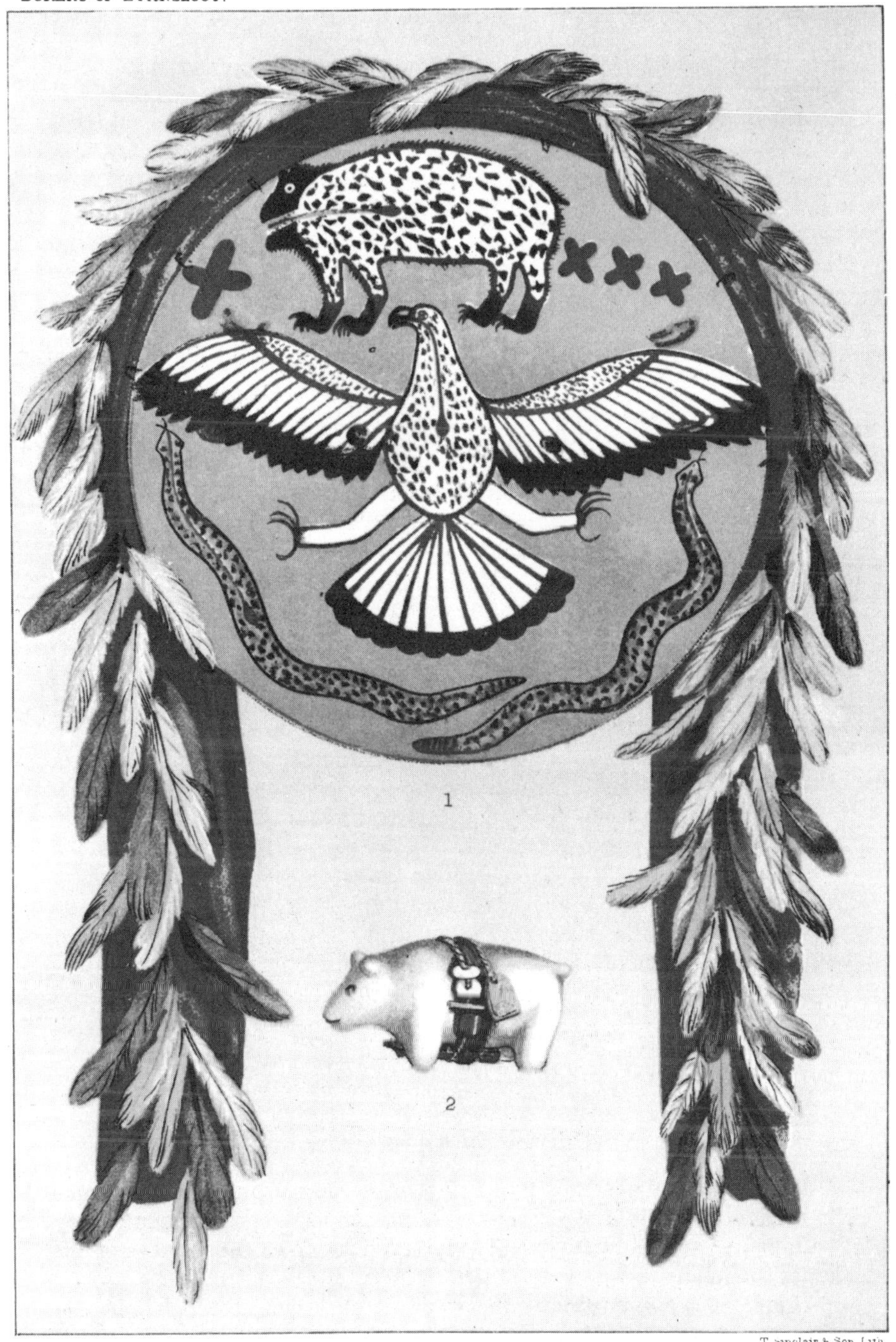

T. Sinclair & Son, Lith.

SHIELD AND FETICH OF THE PRIESTHOOD OF THE BOW.

it. The other was drawn from a sketch made by myself of a fetich in Zuñi.

These fetiches—more usually of the Mountain Lion than of the others; very rarely of the Knife-feathered Demon—are constantly carried by the warriors when abroad in pouches like those of the Hunters, and in a similar manner. They are, however, not returned to the headquarters of the society when not in use, but, being regarded, with the other paraphernalia of their possessor, as parts of his Sá-wa-ni-k'ia, are always kept near him.

RESEMBLANCE TO THE PREY GODS OF THE HUNT.

The perfect fetich of this order differs but little from those of the Hunters, save that it is more elaborate and is sometimes supplied with a minute heart of turkois bound to the side of the figure with sinew of the Mountain Lion, with which, also, the arrow-point is invariably attached, usually to the back or belly. The precious beads of shell, turkois, coral, or black stone, varied occasionally with small univalves from the ocean, are bound over all with a cotton cord. These univalves, the oliva (tsu-i-ke-i-nan-ne=heart shell), are, above all other shells, sacred; and each is emblematic of a god of the order. The wrist badges of the members are also made of these shells, strung on a thong of buckskin taken from the enemy. The arrow-point, when placed on the back of the fetich, is emblematic of the Knife of War (Sá-wa-ni-k'ia ä'-tchi-ën-né), and is supposed, through the power of Sá-wa-ni-k'ia or the "magic medicine of war" (?) to protect the wearer from the enemy from behind or from other unexpected quarters. When placed "under the feet" or belly, it is, through the same power, considered capable of effacing the tracks of the wearer, that his trail may not be followed by the enemy.

THE RITES OF THEIR WORSHIP.

The ceremonial observed by a Priest of the Bow, when traveling alone in a country where danger is to be apprehended from the enemy, may be taken as most illustrative of the regard in which the fetiches of his order are held.

Under such circumstances the warrior takes out his fetich from the pouch, and, scattering a pinch or two of sacred flour toward each of the four quarters with his right hand, holds it in his left hand over his breast, and kneels or squats on the ground while uttering the accompanying prayer:

Si! Lú-k'ia yät-ton-né, hom a-tä-tchú K'ia-pin-á-hâ-i lé-we í-na-kwe
Si! This day, my Fathers, Animal Beings, (all) thus much (by) enemies

pó-ti-tap-té hom ton té-hi-a-na-wé. Ethl tel-i-kwĕn-te thlothl tchu-a
filled through me ye precious render (all do). Not that (in any) way unexpected soever whom (of the)

í-na-kwe hom kwa'-hothl a-k'iá a-tsu-ma-na-wam-i-k'ia-ná. Lú-k'ia yät-
enemy my whatsoever with daring (existence) (pl.) shall. This day

ton-né hom to le'–na
to me ye thus

[At this point, while still continuing the prayer, he scratches or cuts in the earth or sands with the edge of the arrow-point, which is lashed to the back or feet of the fetich, a line about five or six inches in length].

ai'-yäl-la-na-wá. Ethl thlothl-tchu-á í-na-kwe í-pi-kwai-nam-tun a-k'iá
shelter shield (pl.) shall give. Not that whomsoever (of the) enemy pass themselves through to hence

hom ton aí-yäl-la-na-wá. [Here he scratches a second line.] Hâk-ti-
to me ye shelter shield (pl.) shall (give), Tail-long

tä'sh-a-ná, [scratches a third line.] Ä-tchi-a-lä'-to-pá, [scratches a fourth
(Mountain Lion), Knife-feathered,

line] hom ton í-ke-i-nan aí-yäl-la-na-wá.
my ye heart shelter shield (pl.) shall give.

[These lines, although made immediately in front of the speaker, relate to the four points of the compass, the other two regions not being taken into account, since it is impossible for the enemy to bring harm from either above or below the plane on which the subject moves. It may be well to add, also, that four (the number of the true fingers) is the sacred numeral of the Zuñis, as with most all Indian tribes and many other lower races.]

FREE TRANSLATION.

Si! This day, my fathers, ye animal gods, although this country be filled with enemies, render me precious. That my existence may not be in any way so ever unexpectedly dared by the enemy, thus, O! shelter give ye to me (from them). (In order) that none of the enemy may pass through (this line) hence, O! shelter give ye to me (from them). Long Tail [Mountain Lion], Knife-feathered [God of the Knife Wings], O! give ye shelter of my heart from them.

On the conclusion of this prayer the fetich is breathed upon and replaced, or sometimes withheld until after the completion of the war-song and other chants in which the three gods mentioned above are, with others, named and exhorted, thereby, in the native belief, rendering protection doubly certain. I am of course thoroughly familiar with these war chants, rituals, etc. They abound in archaic terms and are fraught with great interest, but belong more properly to another department of Zuñi worship than that of the mere fetichism; as, indeed, do most other recitations, chants, etc., of the War society, in any way connected with this worship.

Before following the trail of an enemy, on finding his camp, or on overtaking and destroying him, many ceremonials are performed, many prayers are uttered, much the same as those described relative to the chase, save that they are more elaborate and more irrelevant to the subject in hand. As with the Hunter, so with the Warrior, the fetich is fed on the life-blood of the slain.